Rhythm of the Gospel

Rhythm of the Gospel

Philip Hacking
and Elizabeth McQuoid

Copyright © 2004 Philip Hacking and Elizabeth McQuoid

10 09 08 07 06 05 04   7 6 5 4 3 2 1

First published in 2004 by Keswick Ministries and Authentic Media
9 Holdom Avenue, Bletchley, Milton Keynes, Bucks., MK1 1QR, UK
and PO Box 1047, Waynesboro, GA 30830-2047, USA
www.authenticmedia.co.uk

The right of Philip Hacking and Elizabeth McQuoid to be
identified as the authors of this work has been
asserted by them in accordance with the
Copyright, Designs and Patents Act 1988.

*All rights reserved. No part of this publication may be reproduced,
stored in a retrieval system, or transmitted in any form or by any
means, electronic, mechanical, photocopying, recording or otherwise,
without the prior permission of the publisher or a licence permitting
restricted copying. In the UK such licences are issued by the Copyright
Licensing Agency, 90 Tottenham Court Road, London W1P 9HE.*

British Library Cataloguing in Publication Data

A catalogue record for this book is available from the British Library

ISBN 1-85078-573-2

Unless otherwise stated, Scripture quotations
are taken from the HOLY BIBLE, NEW INTERNATIONAL VERSION
Copyright © 1973, 1978, 1984 by the International Bible Society.
Used by permission of Hodder and Stoughton Limited.
All rights reserved. 'NIV' is a registered trademark of
the International Bible Society.
UK trademark number 1448790

Cover design by Sam Redwood
Typeset by Temple Design
Print Management by Adare Carwin
Printed and bound by AIT Nørhaven A/S, Denmark

Contents

The aim of this study guide		vii
Introduction		1
1	God's ambassadors	4
2	The ministry of the Spirit	12
3	The treasure of the Gospel	23
4	Strength through weakness	34
5	The eternal perspective	45
6	Ministry of reconciliation	55
7	Gospel appeal	67
8	No compromise	78
9	Ministry of encouragement	91

THE AIM OF THIS STUDY GUIDE

The aim of this study guide is to help bridge the gap between the Bible world and our own. Philip Hacking's commentary digs deep into the second letter to the Corinthians and opens up the world of these first century believers to us. The questions that follow help relate the principles he draws out to our own lives and situations. You can use this guide either for your own devotional time with God or as part of a group. Enjoy your study!

USING THIS BOOK FOR PERSONAL STUDY

Begin by praying and reading through the passage and commentary a number of times before looking at the questions.

You may find it helpful to note down your answers to the questions and any other thoughts you may have. Putting pen to paper will help you think through the issues and how they specifically apply to your own situation. It will also be encouraging to look back over all that God has been teaching you!

Talk about what you're learning with a friend. Pray together that you'll be able to apply all these new lessons to your life.

USING THIS BOOK IN SMALL GROUPS

You will probably only have time to cover one chapter of the study guide per session. However, the guide is designed so that you can decide which chapters you want to use in the sessions you have available

In preparation for the study, pray and then read the passage of Scripture and commentary over a number of times. Use other resource material such as a Bible dictionary or atlas if they would be helpful.

Each week think through what materials you need for the study – a flip chart, pens and paper, other Bible translations, worship tapes?

At the top of each chapter we have stated the aim – this is the heart of the passage and the truth you want your group to take away with them. With this in mind, decide which questions and activities you should spend most time on. Add questions that would be helpful to your group or particular church situation.

Before people come, encourage them to read the passage and commentary that you will be studying that week.

Make sure you leave time at the end of the study for people to 'Reflect and Respond' so they are able to apply what they are learning to their own life situations.

Introduction

Half a century ago as a student I encountered the living, speaking God in a new way.

The venue was Keswick, in a tent that had seen better days, at a Christian Convention even then approaching its century. I was reading history at Oxford and having conflicting thoughts about life after my pleasant academic pursuits. The Civil Service was an option but seemed boring. With my interest in sport and some 'gift of the gab' the exciting possibility was sports commentating and the BBC may have an enquiry letter in the archives.

God had other plans.

At the missionary meeting there was an invitation to personal commitment to full-time service. Without any hesitation Margaret, my fiancée, and I stood to signify our willingness to go wherever and whenever God would finally call us. Months later he was as good as his word and, like Isaiah in the Old Testament, I said, 'Here am I. Send me!' It was a somewhat reluctant response to a call to the ordained ministry in the Church of England. Much has flowed from that personally dramatic moment in an Oxford church. Immediately it meant three letters, to Margaret, to my parents, and to my vicar. Only the last evinced unalloyed joy. But the die had been cast, the church authorities added their *imprimatur* and the Keswick encounter was producing practical fruit.

It is one thing to respond to a dramatic call; it is something else to find the source of inspiration to make the response lasting. In June 1955 I was ordained in Liverpool Cathedral. The laying on of hands was a deeply moving symbol. Of more permanent value was a passage of Scripture recommended to me by an older friend. He directed me to 2 Corinthians 2-7, chapters all about

2 Introduction

mission and ministry, the rhythm of the gospel. It is there I cast anchor and there I still find inspiration for the never-ending task.

Commentators disagree about these chapters. Some see them as an insertion from a previous 'severe' letter from the apostle to a somewhat recalcitrant group of Christians. This is one way of explaining the abrupt change of reference from the absence of his friend Titus to joyous thanksgiving to God (2:12-14). In chapter 7:5-7 Titus reappears with good news from the friends in Corinth. The more logical mind would have brought those two paragraphs together and saved the burst of praise to the end. Our enthusiastic apostle may have worked differently and, by no means out of character, jumped immediately to a paean of praise. Good news of converts quickly leads to thanksgiving for the good news of the gospel and its power.

2 Corinthians 2:14 begins a section which must have had transforming power when it was received by those young Christians in about AD 55. For me, since the defining moment of my ordination, this message of the rhythm of mission and ministry has been my inspiration, primarily in local parochial service in St Helens' city centre and suburban Edinburgh and Sheffield. But the Lord has given me opportunities for wider ministry at home and abroad, mostly in Bible exposition, teaching this way of commitment and service to others. There is no greater privilege than to be thus in the flow of Word and Spirit.

In that unfolding ministry Keswick has been a constant place of refreshment, renewal and recharging. By God's grace, it has always kept a balance in its stress on a life of holiness and a life of service. For holiness without service can become a cloistered virtue and service without holiness can easily lead to exhausted disillusionment. For me, one of the great highlights of leadership at Keswick has been to put the challenge to others, young and not so

Introduction

young, to stand where I stood fifty years ago and start the exciting pilgrimage of mission and ministry wherever and whenever the Lord calls.

CHAPTER 1

God's ambassadors

Aim: To examine the faithfulness of our witness

FOCUS ON THE THEME
Get to know the people in your small group by sharing your experiences of the most pleasant/most pungent smell you've ever smelt and the best/worst letter you've ever received.

Read: 2 Corinthians 2:14-3:3

Paul is a pastors' and preachers' great example. He always blends personal testimony with profound theology. No modern writer has his apostolic authority, but great truths will always have great power when obviously earthed in experience. These chapters in 2 Corinthians are particularly rich in that respect. So the praise that begins this great section in 2:14 stems from news that a group of young disciples are growing up in faith and loving service. Paul's excitement comes from the reminder that his life has been captured by Christ and these Corinthian believers are a living letter composed by Christ which the world could read. Here is the foundation for spreading the gospel in every age, not least in our post-modern, pragmatic world.

God's ambassadors

A LIFE CAPTURED BY CHRIST

Parents constantly complain about their children's inability to remember to say 'thank you'. We should marvel even more at our own slowness to thank others and not least to thank God. When I was visiting a courageous dying ex-climbing man, I learned that the rock on which the final peak climb is secured is often called by the fraternity a 'thank God'. He was waiting for his last pilgrimage climb and the heavenly 'thank God'. He will have reached his goal by now and this time the expression of relief will have no touch of irreverence.

In the rush of life, however, we often forget to express our thanks to God for his interventions in our life. But Paul was gloriously different. He never forgot that he had once been captured by Christ. The picture used in verse 14 is of a Roman general returning in triumph with captured generals shackled in the procession. Paul is not the victor but the enslaved ex-enemy. The major difference is that he is a rejoicing captive.

- *In the difficult times of life how can it be true that 'God always leads us in triumphal procession' verse 14?*
- *Paul thought of himself as a captive. What difference should it make to our lives that we have been captured by Christ?*

Perhaps the nearest modern-day equivalent to this Roman procession is the local football team returning with the cup on an open-top bus to the adulation of crowds of supporters. In 1991, my much loved but often despised Sheffield Wednesday enjoyed such a golden day when returning victorious from Wembley. Sadly it was not possible to drag the mighty Manchester United opponents in chains to make a perfect parallel!

6   *Rhythm of the Gospel*

Traditionally clouds of incense would accompany this triumphal procession. For Paul, this was an analogy of the beautiful aroma of a life that reflects the grace and love of Jesus. The word 'fragrance' is used significantly elsewhere in the New Testament. In Ephesians 5:2, it speaks of the beauty of the sufferings of Jesus on the cross as far as God the Father is concerned; in Philippians 4:18 it is used of the generous giving of God's people; then in John 12:3 the apostle vividly remembers a room filled with the gorgeous aroma of Mary's ointment from her broken flask. The symbolism was not lost on John. Lives and love poured out at the feet of Jesus bring him much joy. Paul's personal testimony of Jesus was not so much of a friend who sorted out all his problems but of a Saviour who at great cost rescued him, and us, from the penalty and power of sin.

● *We don't always smell like the 'aroma of Christ' verse 15. In what circumstances or events do you consistently struggle to be the fragrance of Christ?*

Paul knew from personal experience that a life fragranced with the love of Christ elicited two opposite reactions from two groups of people on completely opposite journeys (v15, also 1 Cor. 1:18, Mt. 7:13-14). The message of the cross and its implications are at the centre of this division. The unconverted Saul of Tarsus had known this battle and now was at the heart of the conflict from the other side. Surprisingly, some church leaders in our day consider the message of life through the blood of Christ a form of primitive religion from which we have grown away. We can never avoid the stumbling block of Calvary.

● *Brainstorm together the contentious issues, apart from the cross, that cause a division between non-Christians and Christians.*

● *In your church, how could you minimise these differences so that the cross was the only issue that caused offence?*

God's ambassadors

In truth, the only message which draws people to Jesus and then to his church will drive others way. To please all is to offer life to none. Wielding such a two-edged sword is an awesome responsibility and 'who is equal to such a task?' In the light of this question, it is certainly appropriate to examine our failings in facing the challenge and standards of our calling. But here Paul has a larger concern. He does not mince his words; the cause is too important for mealy-mouthed words of tolerance. This letter is shot through with denunciations of the false teachers of his day, just as Jeremiah in the Old Testament condemned false prophets 'who prophesy the delusions of their own minds' (Jer. 23:26). Nor was Jesus silent on the subject: he exhorted his disciples to 'watch out for false prophets. They come to you in sheep's clothing, but inwardly they are ferocious wolves' (Mt. 7:15). The greatest dangers for the church lie inside and not outside, and sometimes sadly in those who hold positions of church leadership.

The picture in verse 17 is of peddlers for profit. The language speaks of those who dilute or adulterate wine, not only spoiling the product but making sure of a bigger financial turnover. This is not only true of some of the less scrupulous televangelists who offer easy and popular solutions to life's sicknesses and problems. More subtly, it applies to the ordinary pastor-teacher who is fearful of his security if he dares to speak out on contentious issues and remain firmly true to the Word of God, or who wants to keep the peace at all times. The only way to stand firm in these tempting areas is to remember, 'we speak before God with sincerity like men sent from God' (v17).

● *What practical measures can we put in place to ensure we keep our motives for ministry pure?*

Rhythm of the Gospel

A LETTER COMPOSED BY CHRIST

I have noted a great difference of attitude when applying for positions. It was once very bad form to commend yourself, except very subtly. Today, the candidates are encouraged to sell themselves, to demonstrate quite unashamedly why they are just the person for whom you have been looking. Self-commendation was rife in the Corinthian church (10:12-13). The false teachers boasted in their special visions, revelations and great success statistics. Beware of this danger creeping into our testimonies – the real commendation is in the quality of the product.

Essentially the living local church is the best advert for the gospel. Church notice boards have their place if they are kept tidy and up to date. Gospel car stickers or fish symbols have their value if the driving has a gospel ring about it! Ultimately, however, it is the consistency of the new life and lifestyle of the Christian community that is the letter 'known and read by everybody'. In 1 Corinthians 9:2 Paul calls the church in Corinth 'the seal of my apostleship'. The presence and vitality of a godly fellowship in this wicked city was a powerful testimony to the truth and power of the good news about Jesus and the contemporary work not of ecstatic religions but of the Spirit of God. How different this is from the church as seen by a famous German philosopher, who complained that he could not hear what Christians were saying because their actions were speaking too loudly.

- *How have you noticed people 'reading' your life?*
- *What do people read when they look at your life?*
- *Think about -*
  - *How you treat your employer/employees/customers*
  - *How you talk about your husband/wife in public*

God's ambassadors

- *The relationship you have with your children*
- *What you watch on TV/at the cinema*
- *How you spend your money*

Living letters are a demonstration of the power of the gospel. In Romans 1:16, Paul speaks of the dynamic of this gospel and today's church desperately needs to recapture its confidence in this good news message. Too often we depend upon powerful personalities or the latest gimmick or emotive music to do the work. Times of spiritual revival over the centuries have hinged upon powerful preaching with great conviction. In the Keswick Convention there has been much updating so that the most disheartening comment is, 'Nothing seems to have changed'. Yet with 'power-point' ministry available, genuine Spirit power is still evidenced in the preaching. Styles have changed greatly but not content.

As a teenager, I was an ardent cricketer with great ambitions, far surpassing my academic aspirations. A book by Len Hutton, of Yorkshire and England fame, was my standby. I memorised all the hints and illustrations. Practising in front of a mirror, I was well nigh perfect, but out in the middle on Saturday in front of a huge fast bowler the end product was invariably failure. How I wished I could have the spirit and ability of the master batsman within me. It was not enough to copy and imitate him. More, however, was not possible. In the greater arena of the Christian life things can be different. Imitating Christ is not valueless but we shall always fall short. Yet we have his Spirit working within us, writing this living letter for others to read (v3). That is why Jesus said to his disciples that it was good that he went away (Jn. 16:7). In fact, those same disciples were better men and more effective witnesses after Pentecost than before Calvary. Watching Peter at work in Acts 2-4 is living proof of that truth.

Rhythm of the Gospel

● *In what ways does the Holy Spirit help us be a faithful witness?*

But it was not just the Holy Spirit at work producing these living letters in Corinth. Paul worked hard as well. This letter will later major on the cost of service (6:3-10; 11: 16-29) as a vivid contrast with the superficial and easily popular false teachers. Today we may use modern means of communication to spread the good news but there is no substitute for hard work and sacrifice for the cause.

Some years ago I chaired a large gathering in Sheffield's City Hall to hear Richard Wurmbrand tell his moving and dramatic story. He had spent many years in prison in his homeland, Romania, and shared the gospel with his Communist captors. His life story recounted in *Tortured for Christ* was a best-seller. Many books were sold; hundreds were deeply moved; all of us listened entranced for over an hour. Sensing the mood, I asked for volunteers to help in a visitation scheme to reach untouched thousands in a large ugly building scheme in the city. I was calling for some dedication of time and inconvenience in our busy lives, but nothing compared with Richard's story. My expectations were dashed. Out of the two thousand present, about twenty volunteered. How easy it is to be moved by the accounts of those who suffer for Christ and the gospel, how hard to follow even distantly in their footsteps. What has happened to the spirit which inspired the pioneer missionary C.T. Studd who said, 'Some wish to live within the sound of church or chapel bell. I want to run a rescue shop within a yard of hell?'

● *Think about what your witness is costing you. What sacrifices are you making in terms of your time, money, talents and reputation?*

FURTHER STUDY

In 2 Corinthians 3:1-3 Paul seems to dismiss the idea of recommendation letters but in 8:22-24 he writes one! Look at the contexts of these two passages. Why is Paul's use of the 'letter of recommendation' different? What can we learn from him?

REFLECTION AND RESPONSE

Have some fragranced candles burning as you spend time reflecting on the aroma your life leaves with others. Think over the past week – in what situations have you brought a sweet fragrance? Repent for the occasions where your poor witness for Christ has left a stench. Write a living letter – write down what you would like other people to read from your life. Of the areas where you fall short, choose one and invite the Holy Spirit to start working in you. If it is appropriate, share your letter with the group and pray in twos that your lives would make good reading!

CHAPTER 2

The ministry of the Spirit

Aim: To examine the work of the Holy Spirit in our lives

FOCUS ON THE THEME
Brainstorm as many definitions as you can to describe the Holy Spirit. Think about his role and his work. Try and come up with definitions that a non-Christian would understand.

Read: 2 Corinthians 3:4-18

There is an unusual ornament in our bedroom which gets regularly dusted and returned to its place of honour. It is a miniature cricket bat signed by an Edinburgh youth group of over three decades ago, their less than serious leaving present to a Rector who blended Bible teaching with the creation of a church cricket team of no mean ability. Round the edge of the bat are the three texts that they claimed were my favourite preaching texts. Amongst these is 2 Corinthians 3:18. I have not ceased to count it as one of my chief delights. This verse attracts me by its inclusion of the word 'all'. It speaks of the ministry of the Holy Spirit in every Christian life.

In 2 Corinthians 3:4-18 the whole of the Godhead is at work. Sometimes it is hard to know which person of the Trinity is being highlighted but those blurred edges are significant. Not least the Spirit is working to point us to

The ministry of the Spirit

Christ and to make us more like him. There is no greater privilege, no greater excitement than to be a human instrument in that revolutionary process. I may sometimes have lost heart or grown weary in Christian ministry; I have never lost the thrill of it.

Nor did the apostle Paul ever forget how glorious was the ministry committed to him and ultimately to all gospel preachers. The apostolate died with the first generation of disciples but their commission is still ours. So we share in the very daring contrast Paul makes with the pioneer leader of the people of Israel, Moses himself. It is hard for twenty-first century Gentile Christians to realise just how revolutionary the apostle is being in this chapter. Moses stands unique in history; Paul claims to have a greater, more lasting ministry.

Like Paul, the new age in which we live is the post-Pentecost age with God's Spirit at work. That ministry is gloriously varied. These verses give us a full-orbed insight into that work of the Spirit.

THE SPIRIT OF LIFE

'Religion' is a strange word. On a pastoral visit I came across a man who confronted me angrily with his forceful assertion that 'religion has done more harm than good in history'. My reply left him speechless. I completely agreed. The world-changing events of September 11, 2001 were accomplished in the name of 'religion'. Battles have been fought and murders committed because of religious fanaticism. Not least a religious façade can make people immune to the gospel – nobody knew that better than Paul, alias Saul of Tarsus.

So here in these verses Paul contrasts a religion that kills with a faith that creates. Verse 7 talks of 'the ministry that

14   *Rhythm of the Gospel*

brought death' and this is a reference to the effect of God's law as contained in the Old Testament. There is a moving autobiographical reference in Romans 7:12-14 where Paul demonstrates from personal experience how the law which was meant to bring life had actually the opposite effect, making the genuine seeker only aware of failure and condemnation. Paul's failure to keep the law brought the sentence of death; as he says in verse 6, 'the letter kills'.

Augustine, a great early Christian leader and theologian, recognised the same response to the law in his own life. As a young libertine he loved to flout the law. Faced with a 'trespassers will be prosecuted' notice on an orchard he was determined to perform an act of robbery. He confessed that he did not like that particular fruit but a 'thou shalt not' was sufficient incentive to want to do it. Even the best law flounders because of human sin and rebellion.

● *Think back over your own experience. How did you once 'live by the law'?*

The converted Paul knew that salvation was not dependent on keeping the law or his own achievements. His confidence now comes 'through Christ before God' (v4). And in answering his rhetorical question of 2:16 'who is equal to such a task?' he speaks gladly of not being competent in himself but 'our competence comes from God' (v5). Paul's experience bears witness to the three great foundations of Christian assurance, the three W's – the word of the Father enshrined in inspired Scripture; the work of the Son accomplished in the finished sacrifice on Calvary; and the witness of the Spirit in the believer's heart (Rom. 8: 16).

This confidence in one's salvation leads to effective service. The word 'ministers' in verse 6 is the servant word, used often by Paul – for example three times in

The ministry of the Spirit

Colossians 1, where he refers to the servant of Christ, of the gospel and of the church in that significant order. The Spirit of life gives power to that service. It can be seen most vividly in the experience of Paul's colleague Peter in his pre- and post-Pentecost mode.

● *Think about your ministry – at home, work, church or in the community. Would it be just the same without the power of the Holy Spirit? What checks can you put in place to make sure that the Holy Spirit is central to what you do?*

Some years ago I had an unusual role to play in an evening act of worship. It was a special modern multi-media presentation of the gospel done with much skill and included drama, poetry and dance as well as music and readings. The producers knew that the sermon in Christ Church was non-negotiable. So I was deputed to preach Peter's Acts 2 sermon. I was allowed no Bible, unilaterally not permitted to have notes and certainly quoting my favourite Paul was out of the question. He had not yet been converted!

The experience was quite dramatic for me as I sought to enter into Peter's skin. Why was I so bold in front of these thousands of people when I had quailed before a serving maid and denied Jesus with cursing only weeks before? The answer was overwhelmingly simple. I had repented before the gaze of Jesus; I had met the risen Lord and I had been filled with his Spirit. Here is the secret of a confident ministry and a demonstration of the dynamic rhythm of the gospel.

This ministry is one 'of a new covenant' (v6), words used in hope by Jeremiah centuries earlier and reiterated by Jesus as he instituted the Lord's supper in the upper room (Mt. 26:28). The communion service always proclaims how faithful the Lord is in his promises to us; it should be a place where we renew our loving obedience to him.

Rhythm of the Gospel

THE SPIRIT OF GLORY

'Glory' is one of those biblical words that is hard to define. The psalmist announces that 'the heavens declare the glory of God' and then goes on to explain that the word of God is even more glorious. Pagans, as much as Christians, can exult in the beauty of a sunset or the wonder of a rainbow. I have recently come back from Switzerland and while I was there I also joined the chorus of delight in the symphony of creation. Such a vision of glory speaks of God's power, order and beauty. But here in verses 7-11 Paul refers to a 'fading' glory.

His mind is turning back to a great historic moment in the history of his people, to Mount Sinai and the giving of the Law, arguably the birth of the nation of Israel. The Old Testament records a manifestation of divine activity in fire and earthquake. Here was a message of transcendent power, but it did not last. Even the reflected glory on the face of Moses faded. In a similar way the disciples on the mount of Transfiguration wanted to freeze the event and stay up there. It was not to be. Jesus was on his way to a greater glory.

In 2 Corinthians 4:6 Paul will speak of 'the glory of God in the face of Christ'. The reference is not to the Transfiguration but to the whole life and work of Jesus, who himself pointed to the cross as the moment of supreme glory (Jn. 17:1-5). Here is the one way for human beings to be reconciled to God. No moment can match it and no ministry can be more wonderful than the preaching of it. All other glorious moments pale into comparative insignificance.

● *How can Jesus' gruesome death on the cross be considered glorious?*

The ministry of the Spirit 17

Moses himself knew that the glory he experienced was partial and temporary. In Numbers 11:29 he voiced his longing that one day everyone would know the lasting presence of God's Spirit. It was a prophetic utterance and with the prophets there is always a 'now' and a 'not yet'. Ultimately only in heaven will that glory be seen and shared. That future hope depends completely on the effective work of the cross that leads to the boldness of which verse 12 speaks (cf. Gal. 6:14).

THE SPIRIT OF FREEDOM

'Where the Spirit of the Lord is, there is freedom' (v17). Freedom is a much lauded virtue and most misused. It is not an end in itself. So Paul will argue in his great charter of Christian liberty in the letter to the Galatians that freedom is not to please yourself but to serve the Lord and one another in love (Gal. 5:13).

Paul knew personally the difference freedom in Christ made. Before his conversion he was in bondage to the letter of the law and the many religious observances demanded of such a rigorous well-known Pharisee. He characterised his condition then as blindness, so different from his new boldness in the Christian faith (v12). This man could speak straight to his fellow Jews because he loved them so much. The person who is always tactful and never hurts is the one who does not really care. There is truth in the line of an ancient popular song that says you always hurt the one you love.

So the apostle, knowing his own people and his own unregenerate religious heart, goes back to the picture of Moses and his veil (vv13-17). He recognises the veil that is hard to pierce. It is often the veil of prejudice, pride or intellectualism. I remember arguing long with a university

18 *Rhythm of the Gospel*

graduate about the uniqueness of Christ and the contemporary activity of God's Spirit. The debates were important but the breakthrough only occurred when she found herself praying for the imminent birth of her first child. With the joy of the birth of a baby went the cry of rebirth as she said, 'Now I believe'. God's ways are gloriously unpredictable. Never restrict him to our limited expectations.

● *What are the other veils that the Holy Spirit needs to remove from people's hearts today?*

Opened eyes lead to emboldened lips. Paul's boldness in verse 12 comes from his turning to the Lord and enjoying the freedom that comes from trusting what Jesus has done and not what we try to accomplish (v16-17). There is a wonderful rhythm in this gospel. We come in simple faith; we go with bold convictions. Later Paul will write his *magnum opus* in the letter to Rome with its heart in the great charter of freedom that constitutes chapters 5-8. There you will find freedom from guilt, freedom from sin, freedom from the law's condemnation and freedom from death itself. Could there be anything more magnificently relevant to everyone?

● *Share examples of times when you have experienced the Holy Spirit making you bold.*

● *What can we learn about the purpose and nature of true freedom from the fact that the Holy Spirit is the giver?*

THE SPIRIT OF HOLINESS

We are back to my 'cricket bat' verse. Verse 18 boldly moves away from reference to the great leadership of Moses and Paul with all the comparisons and contrasts and speaks of 'we ... all'. The promise is quite mind-blowing as

The ministry of the Spirit

it speaks of an inward transformation that is the equivalent of the transfiguration of Jesus. The Gospels record that remarkable moment when briefly Jesus shone with divine glory. In some measure that work is happening in my life, with all its imperfections.

We are being transformed into the image of Christ. Clearly we are in the realm of character rather than looks. It is one of the intriguing facts of history that God sent his Son into the world at a time when an accurate representation of his physical appearance could not be conveyed to posterity. The photograph was well in the future! We do, however, have his words and a record of his actions. And that is the image into which we may be formed gradually and sometimes painfully but surely.

- *Think back over the last week. When did you 'reflect the Lord's glory'?*
- *Ponder for a moment on the fact that 'all' believers reflect the Lord's glory. What thoughts come to mind?*

Theologians refer to this process as sanctification and over the centuries it has been the subject of heated debate. Keswick would have been known historically as a Holiness Convention. At times the platform would have proclaimed a message challenging to a crisis sanctification rather like the conversion experience. In recent years we have become, I believe, more genuinely biblical in emphasising the steady process of becoming more like Christ. There is one caveat. In most of our lives there are crises that move the process on, sometimes quite dramatically.

- *What crises have speeded up your own process of sanctification?*
- *Think about your own circumstances now. What struggles, key events, difficult people, or everyday routines is the Holy Spirit using to make you more like Jesus? What lessons does he want you to learn?*

20   *Rhythm of the Gospel*

In this sanctification process there is a vital secret. It stems from the picture of Moses and his unveiled face on the mountain with God. For the Christian it speaks of the vital importance of time spent in the presence of God, as a daily discipline as well as a weekly delight with other believers. I am thankful that as a young Christian I was taught the necessity of the Quiet Time. It can become mechanical and even legalistic and yet in its discipline I have found daily strength. Like any relationship of love, the norm is unexciting but it occasionally moves into beautiful ecstasy.

● *Share practical ideas of how to keep your quiet time fresh and inspiring.*

Such an honest unveiled relationship with a God from whom no secrets are hidden will move from glory to glory. There is no glory quite like spiritual rebirth and yet Christian maturity has its own beauty and elderly saints can be an inspiration to all who are battling along the way. A famous Keswick speaker once confessed that too many believers 'do not finish well'. As we keep in touch with 'the Lord, who is the Spirit' (v17) we should put that statement right, not least by keeping our eyes on the final glory. So Charles Wesley will remind us:

Changed from glory into glory;
till in heaven we take our place;
till we cast our crowns before Thee;
lost in wonder, love and praise.

The ministry of the Spirit

FURTHER STUDY

Look at Philippians 3:3-11. What gave Paul confidence before his conversion? What gave him confidence afterwards? To what extent do we share Paul's perspective?

Corinthians 3:6 talks about us being 'ministers of a new covenant'. What does this mean? What are our responsibilities? Look at Jeremiah 31:31-34, Matthew 26:28, Hebrews 8:7-9;15 for some ideas.

REFLECTION AND RESPONSE

Look back over your definitions of the Holy Spirit. Perhaps they were too limited. Ask God to fill you with more of his Spirit as you reflect on the:

- Spirit of Life – Am I still bound to the law, following men's expectations and trying to please God by my achievements?

- Spirit of Glory – Do I glory in the work of the cross in my life or do I look to others for praise?

- Spirit of Freedom – Have I asked the Holy Spirit to make my witness bold or am I still fearful?

- Spirit of Holiness – To what extent do I reflect the Lord's glory? What is hindering me?

REVIEW OF 2 CORINTHIANS 2:14-3:18

Paul starts this section, 'But thanks be to God...' Paul had suffered many hardships and had even been misunderstood by his own converts in Corinth and yet here he praises God. Re-read these verses, picking out things that Paul would have been thankful to God for. Make a similar list for all the things you are thankful to God for, however great or small. Discuss together how Paul's example of gratitude challenges your own life. What practical steps can we take to become individuals who praise God whatever our personal circumstances?

POINTS TO PONDER
- What have you learnt about God?
- What have you learnt about yourself?
- What actions or attitudes do you need to change as a result?

CHAPTER 3

The treasure of the Gospel

Aim: To examine our role in presenting and preserving the gospel message

> **FOCUS ON THE THEME**
> What are the treasures and family heirlooms you are keeping safe to pass on to the next generation? Are they jewellery, books, or a home? As you think about what is most precious to you, think too about the value you place on the gospel. Is there sufficient evidence that you 'treasure' it? Is it something you are actively passing on to the next generation?

Read: 2 Corinthians 4:1-6

Most homes possess family heirlooms, often providing headaches as well as financial benefits for the next generation. I wonder what my children will do with my treasured copies of *Wisden's Cricketer's Almanac*, since I doubt whether they share my devotion to them. For the Christian there is no treasure like the gospel of Jesus. Or at least that ought to be so. If the gospel doesn't make our pulse race, then what does?

The Greek word for 'gospel' has two children. 'Evangelical' and 'evangelistic' are clearly close relatives. However, they have distinctive connotations that are at times confused. For example, I am often invited to give an 'evangelical' talk at a student gathering when evangelism is the order of the day. 'Evangelical' speaks of standing for

24   Rhythm of the Gospel

the truth of the gospel; 'evangelistic' means taking out that truth. As a Bible-believing Christian I can only preach evangelically and if pressed I confess that I believe that evangelical and Christian are synonymous terms. Such a conviction sounds desperately intolerant. Yet the apostle Paul is clearly on my side and I must also be careful not to neglect the urgency of the evangelistic task.

Paul doesn't give definitions but he does present the boundary markers for the Christian gospel and its proponents. On the one hand, writing from prison in Philippians 1 he demonstrates a gloriously peace-making spirit, announcing that his presence in Rome has caused a stir. Some responded negatively in envy and some positively in love. The large heart of Paul cares little about the motive, since both groups are speaking of Christ. Something of that spirit today would do much to soften the prevalent denominational rivalry.

On the other hand, the same man in a different context could write Galatians 1:8-9. In battling for gospel integrity, he argued that even if an angel from heaven preached a different gospel, he deserved eternal condemnation. The language is strong and repeated. For many this is the unacceptable face of evangelicalism. The apostle would argue, and church history would support him, that any dilution of gospel truth sounds the death knell of the Christian faith. You test a preacher, whatever his credentials, by the yardstick of Scripture; you do not judge Scripture by the latest academic fad or by the statements of the current cleric in high office.

- ● *Which of these elements do you think are part of the 'gospel truth' and which are secondary to the Christian faith?*
  - *The virgin birth*
  - *Jesus' death on the cross for our sins*
  - *The creation of the world in seven days*
  - *Jesus' bodily resurrection*
  - *Jesus' transfiguration*

The treasure of the Gospel

● *Are there any other elements you would like to include in 'gospel truth'? What makes the gospel message so unique?*

Unashamedly the annual Keswick Convention (held in the Lake District) is thoroughly evangelical, recognising differences in church government and peripheral issues. It is a convention as distinct from a conference. The terminology may seem a little archaic but it is a reminder that we convene to hear what God says to us through his word and by his Spirit. We do not meet to confer, exchanging ideas or viewpoints. Increasingly we have added the seminar programme to our platform proclamation without changing our *modus vivendi*. Without arrogance we dare to believe that Paul in the spirit of these chapters would be happy to own us.

The spirit of evangelicalism must always be wedded to the spirit of evangelism. Sadly, there are soundly orthodox fellowships that have lost their outreach dimension. Keswick is not primarily an evangelistic crusade, although year-by-year people come to faith through the teaching and vibrant worship. In Philippians 2:16 Paul uses a verb that can mean either 'hold on' or 'hold out'. He is speaking of the church and its relationship to the 'word of life'. We best preserve the truth of Scripture by sharing it with others and ensuring its spread to the next generation.

● *How would you respond to someone who said, 'I am not a natural evangelist. Apart from explaining a gospel tract how can I "hold out" the "word of life" to my friends and work colleagues?'*

Keswick has many daughter movements in different parts of the world. One of the largest is in South India in Kerala. At the climax of the Maramon Convention there are over one hundred thousand in attendance in a vast dried up riverbed. It is by far the largest congregation to which I have ministered. When I heard how long this Convention

Rhythm of the Gospel

had been in existence, I enquired how they managed in the pre-loudspeaker era. Apparently there were 'interpreters' stationed one third and two thirds distant from the podium. By this staggered route the message eventually reached the back, a red flag was waved and the preacher proclaimed his next word of truth. I wonder how the message got changed in the process. Happily the church does not share that problem historically. We have the Bible's original message to hold out in every generation.

However, there is another balance in these verses. 'Evangelicalism' and 'evangelism' must be wedded; so also must the message and the messenger. Paul constantly reiterates that theme. To the Ephesian elders in a moving farewell speech he urges consistency of life and lip. He urges them to 'keep watch over yourselves and the flock' (Acts 20:28). And he writes to young Timothy to watch his life and teaching closely (1 Tim. 4:16). Before the catchphrase was invented, Paul did believe that in many ways 'the medium is the message'.

THE SAVING TRUTH

Pilate thought that he had the unanswerable question when he asked Jesus, 'What is truth?' Jesus had just claimed to have come into the world to witness to the truth (Jn. 18:37). Then, as now, in a world that is intent on becoming inclusive, such exclusive claims can be a stumbling block to faith. But Paul had no problem with Jesus' claim as he equates 'the truth' in verse 2 with Christ as 'the image of God' in verse 4.

● *How should we respond to those who say that there is some truth in all religions?*

The treasure of the Gospel

This phrase in part goes back to Genesis 1 and its record of the unique creation of mankind as made in God's image. So Jesus became the perfect man, like us in every way except in sin. But the concept goes much further as Paul summarises his preaching in verse 5 as centred on Jesus Christ as Lord, the heart of the original gospel message. It is based on such words of Jesus as in John 14:9 'Anyone who has seen me has seen the Father.' These are audacious words in any culture. For a first century Jew they are incredible. At least his enemies took his claims seriously enough to want to stone him for blasphemy on more than one occasion.

The heart of the gospel is the person of Christ. Theological battles have been fought over the detailed understanding of the relationship between the human and the divine in the personality of Jesus. Blood has been shed over one Greek letter in the credal definition. Perhaps we try too hard to define the indefinable. What matters for our salvation and not just for our orthodoxy is the assurance that Jesus is God. Quite often in the New Testament, quotes about God the Father in the Old Testament are transferred without any hesitation to the person of Jesus, Son of God. A classic illustration is Philippians 2:10, with the promise that every knee will one day bow at the name of Jesus echoing the original promise in Isaiah 45:23 of bowing at God's name.

- *Why does the authority of the gospel hinge on Jesus being both human and divine? Why did he have to be 100 per cent human? Why did he have to be 100 per cent divine?*

All too readily the popular mind balks at this truth, much preferring the more convenient response that Jesus was a good man and a great teacher but not God. It is convenient because it allows me to stand in judgement upon Jesus, to pick and mix from his teachings according to my liking,

28   *Rhythm of the Gospel*

because even great teachers can get it wrong sometimes. To call Jesus Lord or God is to seek to submit to his authority at all times. As an example, the modern mind recoils at the thought of the reality of hell; Jesus often spoke of it. If God has spoken, who can deny it?

If the heart of the gospel is Jesus as Lord, it is also about him being the light of the gospel, illuminating people to the truth. And here in verse 6 there is a double parallel. The 'light shining in the darkness' reminds us of the creation narrative in Genesis 1. For Paul, however, there was a more personal reference as he remembered the events of the Damascus Road and the light, brighter than the noonday sun (Acts 26:13) that brought him temporary blindness but also a spiritual awakening that he compares to a 'new creation' (5:17). This is the transformation which Jesus' truth and light brings, changing unbelievers to believers.

There are, however, other forces at work when the gospel message is proclaimed. Jesus made that clear in his famous parable of the soils (Mt. 13:1-23). It is a parable to explain parables, to demonstrate what happened when even the Prince of Preachers was speaking. The seed was fine and the sower was perfect. Yet the effectiveness of the sowing varied enormously. Not least Jesus spoke of the birds of the air doing their destructive work. These symbolised the activity of Satan, called in verse 4 'the god of this age'. He seeks to make sure that unbelievers are blinded to the truth. Paul had experienced this himself before his conversion. Satan should still be taken seriously. He is at his happiest when we either deny his existence or confine his activities to such obvious stratagems as dabbling in the occult or celebrating Halloween. He is most clever when he dresses up as 'an angel of light' (11:14). The church is his favourite place.

● *Brainstorm together the elements of the gospel that you think Satan would most like to distort.*

The treasure of the Gospel 29

● *Do you recognise any of Satan's subtle distortions in the way you talk about the gospel and represent its values? What would you be tempted to say in the following scenarios? What do you think you really should say?*

— *You want to invite a work colleague to a special 'Visitors Service' in church.*

— *A mother from your child's class at school asks you what your church believes.*

— *You've been invited by the local university Christian Union to give a ten-minute gospel talk. What elements will you include and what will you miss out?*

There is another responsible agent in this passage. Satan blinds the 'minds of unbelievers' verse 4. The word for unbelief occurs fifteen times in the two Corinthian letters, a reminder of its importance in the fight for the gospel and a strong suggestion that unbelievers are responsible for their own condition. Of course, there is a genuine wrestling with the issues of faith found in Scripture itself, but elsewhere Paul will speak of a solemn judgement on all 'who do not know God and do not obey the gospel of our Lord' (2 Thes. 1:8-9).

With these reminders it will never be enough simply to proclaim the truth. Spiritual battles are being fought and can only be won by spiritual weapons (10:3-4). The story of David and Goliath, so beloved of Sunday school teachers of a bygone generation, is actually a great theological parable in action. David's victory is not primarily the goodie over the baddie, or the little guy over the giant. It is the triumph of an active faith in the living God over unbelief in the camp and over-arrogant confidence in worldly strength on the part of the enemy. The battle still rages. The church will not become victorious by apeing the resources of the world but by trusting those weapons that are readily available but all too rarely used, the weapons of prayer.

30 *Rhythm of the Gospel*

THE SOLEMN TRUST

Marketing is a key concept in our society. The first element of marketing strategy is to look to the group we are seeking to impress and fashion things accordingly. Hours of time and vast amounts of money go into this activity. The church must not be blind to this. There is, however, a real problem, since the first direction in which the Christian must look is towards God. So Paul, aware that his ministry is all of God's mercy, consciously seeks to do everything 'in the sight of God' (v2). A great bishop of the Reformation, Hugh Latimer, was preaching before the redoubtable and highly unpredictable Henry VIII. A particular passage seemed somewhat contentious and so Latimer's mind reminded him of the presence of the king. As he was about to draw back from contention, another part of his brain reminded him that he was in the presence of the King of Kings and the message was allowed to hit home.

● *What value, if any, do you think marketing strategies have for shaping our presentation of the gospel?*

Since God cannot be conned we must, like Paul, renounce 'secret and shameful ways' (v2). Those of us who are preachers can be tempted to practise these, for the sake of popularity. Like most preachers, I have suffered agonies over what I considered to be ill-delivered messages and lost sleep in the process. Occasionally comfort came through a testimony from someone who had benefited from that message. More often I had to remind myself in the spirit of 1 Corinthians 4:1-5 that God is the judge, not my very frail spirit.

The marketing strategists then advise us on how best to convey our message. Paul's answer to this is 'to set forth the truth plainly.' The verb speaks of the nature of Christian preaching. It is not primarily good advice on

The treasure of the Gospel

how to live nor is it dialogue to stimulate discussion on different aspects of the truth. There is a place for the discussion group in the life of the church. Our main task is to announce without fear or favour the truth of Scripture, which remains true in every age and culture.

● *In our technological age where people are used to sound bites and small group participation, do you think the traditional sermon still has a place? Explain your answer.*

The noun speaks of the truth and the wise preacher will be unashamed of that which is clearly taught in the Bible and reluctant to be dogmatic on issues where Scripture is silent. The adverb is 'plainly' and that is vital. The more we believe about the truth the more we want it to be understood. Even in Nehemiah 8, the Levites had to spend time interpreting the meaning of the Law to put it in the language of the people. Such was Thomas Cranmer's vision at the Reformation. He wanted the ploughboy to be able to read and understand God's word. In that spirit we have had to update Cranmer's language as well as that of the Authorised Version without for a moment diminishing the truth contained in them. Nor should we allow the language to become childish and banal. Simplicity is not the same as triviality.

To preach Jesus Christ as Lord means that 'we do not preach ourselves' (v5). This is not a call for bland anonymity. Indeed, one definition of preaching is 'truth mediated through personality'. Personality makes for a great richness in true biblical preaching but there also needs to be constant prayerfulness that it does not degenerate into a pulpit ego-trip. To emphasise this further, the 'servant' word in verse 5 is actually the word for 'slaves'. This is the position of the pastor-teacher and it is far removed from the hierarchical structures in so many denominations. Jesus calls us clearly to the servant role

Rhythm of the Gospel

when he speaks of himself in Mark 10:45 as coming not to be served but to serve. Paul wanted to follow this way of service 'for Jesus' sake'. Only then can a pastor keep faithful when his ministry seems rejected or just unappreciated.

● *It isn't politically correct to talk of someone being a 'slave' but how does the term give us a right perception of our role?*

The truth of the gospel is a treasure to be kept for and given to the next generation. Most people wisely give much thought to their Last Will and Testament, making sure that what is left behind is best used. Christians should be particularly concerned at this level. Even more thought should be given to our responsibility in handing on intact the good news of Jesus and his love to the coming generation.

FURTHER STUDY

We have already seen how the promise in Isaiah 45:23 speaking of God was transferred in Philippians 2:10 to refer to Jesus. Can you give other examples where quotes, titles, roles given to God the Father in the Old Testament are applied to Jesus in the New Testament?

Look at Mark 4:15, 2 Corinthians 11:14, 12:7. What is the current role of Satan? How does he still wield power if Colossians 2:13-15 is true?

REFLECTION AND RESPONSE

As a group, brainstorm your 'Last Will and Testament'. Write down all the items in the spiritual legacy that you want to leave the next generation – your own children and the ones in your youth group or Sunday school class. Are you protecting this spiritual legacy in the same way you're protecting your heirlooms, are you giving it the

The treasure of the Gospel

attention you're giving your nest egg? What steps do we need to take as individuals, a local church, and a universal church to ensure that the gospel and its values are safe in our hands?

CHAPTER 4

Strength through weakness

Aim: To re-examine the paradoxes of the gospel message

FOCUS ON THE THEME
The gospel message is full of paradoxes – unexpected heroes, unpromising strategies and unlikely outcomes. Think back to the last film you saw or book you read. What were some of the storylines that shocked you because of their surprising twists and strange endings? What makes the gospel account the best story of all?

Read: 2 Corinthians 4:7-18

Bible translations abound. In this book we use the New International Version but I was nurtured on the Authorised Version and still instinctively quote from it. There can be a fascination in tracing phrases and their updating. 2 Corinthians 4:7 talked in AV language about 'earthen vessels'; NIV prefers 'jars of clay'. I have warmed to a contemporary suggestion of 'plastic bags'. The ubiquitous plastic bag of our supermarket world fits the analogy well. Paul is contrasting the value of the treasure with the worthlessness of the container. The humble plastic bag often hides a purchase of considerable worth.

There is more significance in the analogy. Our first century householder would seek to fool the thief by deliberately concealing treasure in a humble container. We

Strength through weakness 35

are about to be reminded that the gospel servant is of little worth in himself. Yet the message he proclaims is the greatest treasure in the world.

This letter is written in the context of false teachers who boasted of gifts and achievements. But these verses in chapter four not only contrast the frailty of the messenger with the glory of the message, they show how one grows out of the other. Verse 17 speaks of these troubles achieving glory. All this stands in vivid contrast with normal secular expectations and superficial Christian priorities.

Some parts of the church have been going recently through a new craze, based on a long-forgotten prayer of the Old Testament – the prayer of Jabez. This is tucked away in long lists of names in 1 Chronicles 4:10 and has its own beauty. It reads; 'Oh, that you would bless me and enlarge my territory. Let your hand be with me, and keep me from harm so that I will be free from pain.' We have the biblical assurance that God answered the prayer very positively and less sure anecdotal evidence that repeating the prayer today can be effective. Many of us find it strange that this tiny prayer has been given such prominence today when Scripture remains silent as to its continuing significance. More seriously, it suggests a state of mind that looks for personal prosperity and security rather than effectiveness in service and likeness to Christ. Certainly Paul's own priority was not his own blessing but to let God's strength and power be showcased through his weakness.

POWER THROUGH FRAILTY

Our contemporary society is characterised by pressure, however subtle. In a recent discussion with a medical consultant I was assured that retirement can actually bring more stress than work, not least because we are conditioned

36   *Rhythm of the Gospel*

by an attitude which is more concerned with doing rather than being. All too often our first question on being introduced to a person is about what they do in life. Paul knew what it was to be under pressure and almost unbearable stress. He described himself as 'hard pressed on every side' (v8). There follows a list of contrasts between the constant pressures and the amazing resilience he discovered (vv8-9).

● *Taking examples from your own life, continue Paul's list in verses 8-9. Use his format and style.*

Far from being supermen and women these early Christians knew their frailty. The only secret of the survival of the church lay in the 'all surpassing power of God' which enabled the church to snatch victory out of the jaws of defeat (v7). So Moffat translates the concluding phrase of verse 9 'knocked down but not knocked out'. For Paul this was no colourful metaphor. At Lystra in Acts 14 he was stoned and left for dead but bounced back, resumed his ministry, even returning to the place of stoning to care for the young church there.

This principle has often been worked out in church history. The forces of evil have knocked down church communities but never knocked them out. Certain church groups and even denominations can disappear and die because of heresy and apostasy within and we must ever be on the alert. Yet the church will ultimately triumph. The book of Daniel has always encouraged the saints of God. Daniel and his friends were not saved from going through the fire and the lions' den but they were not only kept safe within the testing environment, they actually met God in a new way in the persecution and made real, if temporary, inroads into the pagan religions of their exilic homeland.

● *Think through your own weaknesses. How has God used them to make you more like Jesus? If it is appropriate, share your answers in twos.*

LIFE THROUGH DEATH

As a young English minister learning to adjust to Scottish ways, culture, and church affairs in the sixties, I became acquainted with a remarkable Church of Scotland minister in Glasgow, Reverend Tom Allan. His book *The Face of My Parish* was a great inspiration to me as I planned my parochial priorities. I heard him speak of his conversion to Christ when he was already training for the Presbyterian ministry; I was impressed by his willingness to support Billy Graham when many of his ecclesiastical contemporaries were sceptical; not least I was excited by his outreach ministry in the heart of the city amongst the most unlikely. So his early death at the age of 47 hit me hard.

Often I had heard wise pundits prophesy that his pace of life was dangerous and yet his selfless dedication challenged me. I think of him when I read the literal translation of 2 Corinthians 4:10 – 'we always carry around in our body the dying of Jesus'. Of Paul, as of Tom Allan, it could have been said that the work was 'gradually killing him'. This is the principle reiterated in verse 11 that says we are actually being 'given over to death.' We are privileged to share the way of the cross so that we can also know the reality of his resurrection. This is part of the rhythm of gospel ministry and a truth that Paul expounds in Romans 6.

The phrase 'given over' in verse 11 is used elsewhere in the New Testament of Jesus being handed over by Judas, Caiaphas and Pilate to his ultimate fate. Such is the close relationship between the Saviour and his servants. We are being 'given over to death' just as Jesus was, we follow in his footsteps. Indeed, in Philippians 3:10 Paul explains it is his great ambition to get to know Christ 'and the power of his resurrection and the fellowship of sharing in his sufferings'. The order is surely significant as well as

38   *Rhythm of the Gospel*

surprising. A living relationship with the Lord starts with an awareness of the reality of his risen power; only later comes the awareness of what it may cost to follow him. At least that was Paul's Damascus Road experience.

● *Paul says he wants to 'know...the fellowship of sharing in his sufferings'. How do you cope with suffering? Does this passage offer you any comfort or hope?*

In verses 11-12 the promise of life in our mortal body has a double reference. In part it is a present reality; we come alive at the moment of conversion. Yet there is also a strong future promise here. I knew of a fine if eccentric gentleman who decided to give his own funeral oration; tape-recorded in advance, of course. It began 'Welcome to this service. You all thought I was dead. I have never been more alive.' The idea was quaint, the thought eminently biblical with its emphasis on the wonder of the resurrection of the body. It was this conviction that nerved the apostle for his many pressures and persecutions (vv8-9). He could speak of facing death daily (1 Cor. 15:31). Writing from Ephesus, he spoke in the next verse of fighting with wild beasts, either literally or metaphorically; just as in 2 Corinthians 1:8-9 he spoke of having the sentence of death, probably more in terms of acute depression than a legal fear, hanging over him.

● *Look at verses 10-11. The word 'body' is repeated three times. Why does Paul think that this term is so significant?*
● *Look at verse 14. Why is the literal resurrection of Jesus so important to the gospel message?*

Because we live in a 'now' generation that demands instant answers and instant pleasures, we desperately need the corrective of the New Testament balance with its 'now' and its 'not yet' when it speaks of the kingdom of God. There are spiritual realities that will only be ours in

Strength through weakness 39

heaven. Our age badly needs a dose of teaching on heaven to save us from unrealistic and unbiblical expectations and to inject instead the wonders of that glorious hope when death will finally be swallowed up in life, rather than the reverse that is the fear of all unbelief.

● *We need 'teaching on heaven to save us from unrealistic and unbiblical expectations.' What unrealistic and unbiblical expectations do you think this generation of believers have? How would teaching about heaven help?*

BLESSING THROUGH SACRIFICE

There is a vital spiritual principle outlined in verse 12, which is the key to the next stage in Paul's argument. 'Death is at work in us, but life in you.' This lies behind the whole ministry of Jesus, the Suffering Servant, who gave his life as a ransom for many (Mk. 10:45). In the fullest sense, that was a unique ministry but Jesus did call his disciples to follow in his example, even using the analogy of taking up the cross. In Jesus' day, the cross was not shorthand for carrying a burden but the prelude to death. Thus a condemned criminal carried his own cross to the place of execution. In Christian discipleship, there is a personal 'death' involved.

● *What daily dying do you do? Are you aware of carrying your cross on a daily basis?*

We must never spiritualise away that theme of sacrifice. Paul ends one of his most dynamic letters with the testimony 'I bear on my body the marks of Jesus'(Gal. 6:17). This is no reference to magical stigmata, I believe, as some have claimed. It simply refers to the marks of the whippings, the deprivation, and the beatings endured in the cause of the gospel. The cry of one of the early church

40 *Rhythm of the Gospel*

leaders that, 'The blood of the martyrs is the seed of the church' rings true across the centuries. Some years ago I stood in a tiny graveyard in the north of Nigeria, having just preached to an eager and large group of young believers. As I read the inscriptions of missionaries and their children who lost their lives to help found a church in that area, I remembered those words and gave thanks. Because of their ultimate sacrifice, these Christians were alive.

Pastoral ministry can be very costly. One of the privileges of Keswick ministry is to bring encouragement and a continuing challenge to pastors who come to the Convention often weary and sometimes dispirited. Several times there I have recounted the moving story of one of my heroes, William Grimshaw, vicar of Haworth in Yorkshire. Grimshaw was a dedicated evangelical who remained within the Church of England in the early days of Methodism, though very much at one with the Wesleys. On one occasion he had finished a gruelling Sunday with several services inside and outside his church, when he remembered a farmer several miles away, near to death and without the assurances of faith. So immediately the weary preacher mounted his horse to visit and pray with his parishioner. How many of us modern ministers, after two Sunday services, would have driven in the car to visit someone that same evening? Perhaps we do not have the same conviction about the solemnity of dying without faith and perhaps we have learned to take things more easily.

● *In what areas do you think the church has become complacent? What difference can individual Christians make?*

There is no shortcut to fruitful ministry. The psalmist speaks of sowing in tears and reaping in joy and Jesus bids us become a grain of wheat falling into the ground to die in order to bear fruit (Ps.126:5; Jn. 12:24). Vividly Scripture

Strength through weakness   41

demonstrates this theme as Stephen, the first Christian martyr, goes to his death because of his courageous and prophetic preaching. As he does so a young man called Saul, convinced that Stephen was wrong and yet unable to defeat him in debate, holds the coats of those who are stoning Stephen. Soon that same Saul, on the road to Damascus, will acknowledge the lordship of Jesus, thus following in the martyr's footsteps. Death in one brings life to the other.

The ultimate purpose of all Christian ministry is summed up in verse 15. There is a constant desire to reach more people, to cause more tanks to overflow and supremely to bring more glory to God. Here is the rhythm of the gospel again. Effective outreach brings greater blessings inwards. The work can indeed be costly but it brings great rewards. The first bishop of Liverpool, the famous writer and evangelical stalwart, J. C. Ryle, wrote that, 'no converted man is happy to go to heaven alone'. He will always be eager to lead others in the same direction, whatever it may take.

GLORY THROUGH SUFFERING

2 Corinthians 4 ends triumphantly, with its contrast of present testing and often weakness with future glory. In fact one grows out of the other. The contrast is more between present and future than between body and spirit. Paul was not a psychologist ahead of his time; he was a believer with a right perspective. In my schooldays I was a dunce in the art class, not least because I never could understand how to achieve perspective in my 'masterpieces'. There was a trick of the trade by raising a pencil to the horizon but it always eluded me. There are no such tricks to learning perspective in life but there is a great secret.

Rhythm of the Gospel

For most of us, our present troubles occupy our waking (and even sleeping) thoughts. Paul sees these troubles as 'light and momentary' when compared with the glory of heaven that is eternal and 'weighty' (v17). Indeed the original Hebrew word for 'glory' means 'heavy and weighty'. Our perspective depends on where we focus our eyes. On my first visit to Switzerland I had to go against all my natural inclinations by descending into the abyss by chair lift. I discovered that the secret of safe arrival was by keeping my eyes fixed on the glorious mountain peak. Looking upwards meant safe travel and a quieter heart until my feet were on firm ground again. Therein lies a parable that Paul would probably have enjoyed.

As verse 18 explains, it matters supremely where we fix our gaze. The writer to the Hebrews gave a similar challenge to fix our eyes correctly. The phrase occurs in Hebrews 12:2 where we are exhorted to 'fix our eyes on Jesus', seen in his glory but bearing the marks of his sacrificial death. Some years ago I preached at a Boys' Brigade service in Northern Ireland, somewhat ironically because as a boy I had been literally thrown out of my local battalion for consistent insubordination. However, I was able to make amends on this occasion, preaching from the Hebrews' text. In preparation for the service I had taken the salute at the march past of these hundreds of boys. At the cry of 'Eyes right' I knew I had my text for the day. In terms of Hebrews 12, we need our eyes on the heroes of the faith outlined in chapter eleven, on the course we have to run, on our own spiritual condition, but above all on Jesus who assures us that the reward of heaven makes the price we may pay now for faithfulness trivial by comparison (see Rom. 8:18).

● *How do you keep your eyes 'fixed on Jesus'? List all the practices and activities that you include in your weekly routine.*

Strength through weakness 43

● *What advice would you give to someone who had lost their focus on Jesus and was trying to get back on track?*

Strangely we are often muted about heaven at a time when death seems the only enemy left to be conquered, the great unmentionable subject of today. Perhaps we are hesitant because honesty about the promise of heaven will lead inevitably to the equally biblical teaching about hell. Paul has no such inhibitions and will go straight on to the eternal perspective with the words 'Now we know' in 5:1. This world and its pressures will only finally make sense in the context of eternity. A little homesickness for heaven would not come amiss.

FURTHER STUDY
In 2 Corinthians 4:16 Paul writes 'we are being renewed day by day'. Look at these other references – Romans 12:2, Psalm 51:1-2, 10, Isaiah 40:31. What principles do they teach us about how we can be 'renewed day by day'?

REFLECTION AND RESPONSE
Imagine an old-fashioned set of kitchen scales, the kind that measured using weights and balances. In your mind put on one side of the scales all the frailty, death, sacrifice and suffering that you have experienced in your own life. On the other side imagine all the power, life, blessing and glory that God promises us. Re-read 2 Corinthians 4:7-18 and pick out phrases about God and what he is doing on our behalf to add to this side of the scales. Praise God together for the truth that 'Our light and momentary troubles are achieving for us an eternal glory that far outweighs them all' (v17).

REVIEW OF 2 CORINTHIANS 4:1-18
In 4:1 and 4:16 Paul writes 'Therefore we do not lose heart'. Read back over the chapter and pick out all the difficulties that the apostle

Rhythm of the Gospel

experienced from both inside and outside the Christian community. What motivated Paul to keep on going, why did he not 'lose heart'? Think about how he viewed his struggles and how he kept his focus on God. What can we learn from Paul's example?

- Are there other practices you could put in place in your life so that in difficult times you won't 'lose heart'?
- Have you got a friend you could pray with?
- Have you got a favourite worship tape or CD you could play?
- Have you got a favourite portion of Scripture that you could meditate on?
- Have you got a special place you could go, a place you could walk and enjoy the beauty of creation?
- Have you got someone else you could help out and show love to?

POINTS TO PONDER

- What have you learnt about God?
- What have you learnt about yourself?
- What actions or attitudes do you need to change as a result?

CHAPTER 5

The eternal perspective

Aim: To re-examine our priorities and values in the light of eternity

---

FOCUS ON THE THEME
What are you hoping for? List the top three things you're hoping for. It could be to have a baby, for your spouse to become a Christian, or to get promotion at work. Where on your list would you rank your longing for heaven?

Read: 2 Corinthians 5:1-10

The Puritans had their quaint sayings that were often trenchantly true. One of them was that putting a penny close to the eye could keep out the light of the sun. Some immediate problem, however trivial, may prevent me enjoying blessings that seem distant just at the moment. Jonah the prophet discovered that truth and was gently rebuked by God. The sun was beating down and he had been divinely protected by the shade of a plant; then the plant died and he grumbled at God's lack of care. The fact that thousands of Ninevites had been saved from destruction seemed inconsequential. In the light of his momentary inconvenience Jonah had lost all perspective. In 2 Corinthians chapter 5:1-10 Paul wants to direct us to

46 *Rhythm of the Gospel*

some plain teaching about heaven, a theme which is the secret of his confidence in all circumstances.

● *What are the immediate problems that are causing you to lose your eternal focus?*

Confidence in the future will always affect life in the present. Equally, assurance of the reality of God and the heavenly kingdom puts earthly realities in true perspective. Thus the early patriarchs of the Old Testament were characterised as building their altars and pitching their tents. Both verbs and nouns are significant. Material possessions were temporary and the marks of worship permanent. How very different is the life of faith for many today. Hebrews 11 should be regular compulsory reading with its reminder of those who lived and died seeking a city to come. Without the reality of heaven, life for the believer will always be incomplete.

In the New Testament these truths have an added dimension in the promised return of Christ. With that hope, we should be pure as Christ is pure and live holy and godly lives (1 Jn. 3:3, 2 Pet. 3:11). When Paul speaks here about heaven there is no touch of morbidity, no death wish, rather there is inspiration for living and active service. When he speaks of groaning in verse 2 this is not the noise of pain but of unfulfilled anticipation. Our society has made death the great unmentionable and tragedies seem to hit us all the harder because of this. So Paul's perspective comes with refreshing clarity.

LIVE IN HOPE

Hope is what makes the future real in the present. For many people the moment of deepest depression is when there seems no future to live for. It may come when the children finally leave home, when a lifetime's work is done, when a

The eternal perspective

deeply loved husband or wife dies. There is also the challenge of persevering in hope when God's promise seems desperately delayed. The supreme biblical illustration of this is Abraham and Sarah awaiting the promised gift of a son until they were well past childbearing age. Hope is a powerful, biblical decision of the will.

In this chapter Paul will liken our earthly body to a tent, an image used also in 2 Peter 1:13-14. It is a humble reference; it reminds us of the transience of life on earth and prompts us to hope for something better. There is a phrase often used in the United States of the current vice-president being 'only a heart's beat away from the presidency'. More relevantly we are all only a heart's beat away from eternity. That came home to me most vividly in 1989 when I was present at my favourite football ground in Sheffield at what has become known as the Hillsborough disaster, when over ninety Liverpool football fans were killed in a tragic accident. These were mostly young people and as I spent time counselling people at the ground in the aftermath, the enormity of the message hit me. Here were young folk in the prime of life hopefully watching their team get to Wembley and suddenly faced with the reality of eternity. Our tents are very frail and at the mercy of illness and accident. We must keep our 'tents' as well preserved as possible but be wisely aware of their fragility.

In contrast, Paul can speak of 'a building from God, an eternal house in heaven, not built by human hands' (v1). He is anticipating, hoping, for that future day and uses language elsewhere employed in the description of the Temple. The Jerusalem Temple, even in its glorious Solomonic form, was only a limited parallel of the glory of heaven. In a similar way, our bodily tents are a pale reflection of our heavenly bodies. And here Paul explains the uniquely Christian concept of the resurrection of the body, as distinct from pagan belief in the immortality of the soul (vv2-4). In Athens

48   *Rhythm of the Gospel*

Paul had to face sneering and contempt as he battled for the Christian view, based on the historic truth of the resurrection of Jesus (see Phil. 3:21). In more modern times, this bodily resurrection theme battles with often ill-defined but widely held views of re-incarnation.

● *If Christians are going to get resurrection bodies why should we look after our earthly bodies now? Look at Romans 6:12-14, 12:1; 1 Corinthians 6:15, 9:27; 1 Timothy 4:8.*

With this conviction Paul had a personal battle: he longed to move straight into his resurrection body without any intermediate state after death. In 1 Corinthians 15:51-52 he had dramatically assured his readers that 'we will not all sleep but will all be changed' – the truth that all believers will share in the great resurrection moment at the return of Jesus. Now he hopes, forlornly as we now know, still to be alive on that day. However he has no doubt of the truth of verse 4b that the mortal will be swallowed up by life, the exact opposite of the worldly fear that death will finally swallow up life's achievements.

Inevitably there is some vagueness when we move from time into eternity where there can be no 'now.' So we hold together these two great New Testament assurances that when a believer dies, they are 'with Christ which is far better' (Phil. 1:23) and that one day the dead and those alive in Christ will meet together with the returning Christ and then be 'forever with the Lord' (1 Thes. 4:16-18). Beyond that there can be gentle agnosticism. I like to picture it as sleep, which is a New Testament word for the death of the believer. In good sleep the hours pass without our conscious awareness. For the original Christians of the first century, as for their successors in the twenty-first, after death the next moment will be the Parousia, Christ's coming in majesty. In the meantime, awaiting the resurrection body, the believer's soul is safe with Christ.

The eternal perspective

In verse 5 Paul goes on to speaks of the foundation on which we build our hopes for the resurrection and our eternity with Christ. This foundation for our hope is in the plan and purpose of God in his creation and redemption. Not least God has given the Holy Spirit as a down payment, assuring us of our final inheritance in heaven. The Greek word here is 'arrabon' which in modern Greek is used of the engagement ring. There is a close parallel here. When as a fairly impecunious student I became engaged and gave Margaret a ring as a symbol of my love and loyalty, it was an assurance that the second ring would follow in due course. In our case that was a full three years later as I was called to the ordained ministry, necessitating a waiting period. The costly ring was always on her finger as a proof that the promise would eventually be fulfilled.

In the much higher spiritual equivalent, the gift of the Spirit to the believer, only possible because of the costly sacrifice of Calvary (Jn. 7:39), becomes the pledge of that heavenly relationship seen as 'the wedding feast of the Lamb'. In days of doubt we remember that the one who gave his own Son and then sent his Spirit will not fail to finish the task and take us to heaven. This never becomes complacency but it does undergird that precious and often lacking gift of assurance. For the Christian, this assurance comes from the word of the Father, always trustworthy; the work of the Son, completely finished; and the witness of the Spirit, inwardly consistent

- *How does the Holy Spirit give us assurance of our eternal security?*
- *In times of doubt and difficulty, how have you gained assurance of your salvation? Share together examples of people, events, and passages of Scripture that have been helpful.*

50   *Rhythm of the Gospel*

Here Paul twice speaks in verses 6 and 8 of his confidence. This is the effect of hope in life and the fruit of living by faith and not by sight, in the classic statement of verse 7. So in Scripture the great men and women were called to act in faith where they could not possibly see. This does not mean they had to anaesthetise their minds. Faith is not an enemy of reason; Paul often spoke of the need to renew one's mind and he prayed for the gift of knowledge and wisdom. With a faith firmly rooted in the history of the birth, life, death and resurrection of Jesus of Nazareth, the use of the mind in study is clearly central. Hebrews 11:1 actually gives us the perfect definition of faith as 'being sure of what we hope for and certain of what we do not see'. Illustrations of that thought-through hope-filled confidence called 'faith' abound in that dramatic chapter. Noah obeys God and builds an ark without any physical evidence of a flood; Abraham offers Isaac, his son of the promise as a sacrifice when it apparently contradicts the whole promise scenario; Moses chooses to be identified with the Hebrew slave population, when he could have been a pampered highly educated Egyptian prince.

Living by faith and not by sight is particularly relevant when considering the reality of heaven. That is very much the theme of the often sentimentalised and misunderstood 1 Corinthians 13. One of the great arguments of the chapter is that here on earth we see 'but a poor reflection as in a mirror'. The word actually means that we see 'enigmatically' or like a riddle. This is the limit of our concept of heaven now but 'then we shall see face to face'. Only in heaven will there be perfect knowledge. It is therefore not surprising that Paul looks forward to that day when he will be 'at home with the Lord'. So faith and hope dwell together and ensure that love triumphs.

● *In the Christian world 'living by faith' is often the term for being in ministry without a guaranteed salary. Brainstorm the concepts and promises that the Bible asks all believers to accept by faith.*

● *Take one of these concepts or promises and discuss together how it should impact your life on a daily basis. How would it affect the decisions you make, your lifestyle or attitudes?*

LIVE IN HOLINESS

I recently came across one of those theological phrases that lose their challenge in the mouthful of words. It said, 'The eschatological indicative is always followed by the moral imperative.' When I quote this from the Keswick platform it raises no cheers and it evokes few nods of agreement. It is a complicated way of saying that the truth of Our Lord's return should always lead to a command for action now. Perhaps I had better stick with our Lord's call to 'watch and pray' after his clear teaching about the future and his return (Mt. 26:41). So Paul will insist in verse 9 that the thought of final glory drives him to a constant desire to please the Lord on earth, as he most certainly will do in heaven.

● *Brainstorm together the different reasons Christians get involved in church ministry.*

● *Why is it crucial that in ministry our central goal is to please Christ (v9)?*

One of Jesus' most searching parables about the future with its present implications is his story of the talents and the possibility of those great words of welcome 'Well done good and faithful servant.' Such a welcome presupposes that the servant has pleased his absent master. One of the most powerful sermons on this parable was preached in Keswick by George Hoffman, founder of Tearfund. Tragically, George was killed only weeks after preaching the sermon. He ended a very dramatic challenge to

52

Rhythm of the Gospel

committed service by asking the pertinent question as to how the Lord would respond to us if that day became this day. Would the risen Jesus say 'Well done' or would he quizzically ask us 'Well...??' The clear innuendo was that, for many of us, there are serious question marks about the reality of our call to please the One who lived and died that we might have eternal life.

Our responsibility becomes (in verse 10) our accountability. This verse cannot be construed in a way that denies justification by grace alone, grace that could give life to a dying penitent thief. Yet there are sufficient passages to warn us against complacency. Our faith alone responds to his grace alone but such faith will never be alone. New Testament teaching is clear – look at Ephesians 2:8-10 and Matthew 25:31-46. The latter verses give solemn teaching that what we do to others is measure of what we do to the Christ whose name we honour. As an old evangelical song goes:

> I would not work my soul to save,
> for that my Lord has done
> but I would work like any slave
> for love of his dear Son.

There are inevitably some mysteries about heaven and our entry into it. Wholehearted acceptance by our gracious Lord does not preclude the testing of the quality of our Christian service. In 1 Corinthians 3:10-15 there is a sobering passage concerning testing by fire to prove how effectively we have built upon the one sure foundation. To have assurance of one's final destiny can and should go alongside a healthy fear of failing to please the Lord on that day of reckoning. Even the ardent Paul feared that he might be a 'castaway' in spite of having preached to others.

The eternal perspective

- *How do you feel knowing that you will one day appear before the judgement seat of Christ (v10)?*
- *Do you think in heaven it will be possible to experience fear or a sense of disappointment at failing Jesus? Use other Bible passages to support your answer.*

Here we are on the edge of Paul's classic exposition of motivation for mission (5:11-6:2). We may rightly stress that becoming a Christian makes sense of and gives spice to this life. Yet ultimately it is the eternal perspective that drives the evangelist on, in spite of disappointments along the way. I discovered this when leading a Lenten series of seminars on the theme of evangelism. All seemed agreed on the principle and paid lip service to its importance but obviously were content to do nothing about it. In a moment of inspiration I decided to speak on heaven and hell. Suddenly it all came alive, producing a great division of opinion that demonstrated where the fault-lines lay. Those who believed in the clear biblical teaching, not least on the lips of Jesus, concerning an eternal parting of the ways were the ones motivated against all odds to take out the good news of Christian hope. To have a vague belief in universalism assuming that all reach heaven eventually made evangelism an optional extra. How different with the apostle!

- *Think about five friends or colleagues who do not share your hope of heaven. Commit to praying for them regularly that one day they would come to know Jesus personally and spend eternity with him.*
- *What difference would having an eternal perspective make? Think about:*
  - *The way you treat your work colleagues*
  - *Your relationship and expectations of your children*
  - *Your efforts in evangelism*
  - *Your view of work*
  - *Your ministry in the home/church/community*

Rhythm of the Gospel

54

- *What practical steps can you take to adjust your focus and regain your eternal perspective?*

REFLECTION AND RESPONSE

Will God say to you 'Well...' or will he say 'Well done, good and faithful servant'? Perhaps focus on an empty chair in the room as you imagine appearing before the judgement seat of Christ. Confess your sins and failures quietly to him now. Think back over the hopes that you shared at the beginning of this session. Bring them to God, rededicating yourself to him and his service. Think about what attitudes and behaviour you need to change so that you can say with sincerity 'I make it my goal to please him.' Repeat this phrase throughout the week, using it as a prayer as you respond to different people and situations

CHAPTER 6

Ministry of reconciliation

Aim: To examine our new status and ministry as believers

FOCUS ON THE THEME
What have been the 'red letter' days in your life: days where something happened that changed its course? It could be your wedding day, the day you started a new job, had a baby or met someone who turned out to have a big influence on you. Do you remember the day you became a Christian? Whether you remember the exact day or not, it was a 'red letter' day because you acquired a new status of being 'in Christ' and a new ministry of reconciliation.

Read: 2 Corinthians 5:11-21

In 2 Corinthians 5:11-21 Paul threads together deep theological concepts with his own moving testimony. The paragraph is born out of the thought in verse 10 of the judgement seat of Christ, where all must eventually appear. And it will lead to the urgency of chapter 6 with its call to respond. These verses encapsulate the central point of the letter and demonstrate once again the 'rhythm of the gospel.'

To mark the importance of this theme Paul rises to a great exaltation of style. Neither in writing nor in preaching should beauty of language be the highest goal.

Rhythm of the Gospel

56

Nor is crude banality excused in the search for contemporary relevance. Yet there is no loss of forceful clarity in the apostle's message. With the dignity of an ambassador he describes himself as a slave to the message of Christ's love (vv14,20). And he speaks again of the paradox of the power of the gospel centred on the weakness of a crucified saviour (vv14,15,21).

THE MOTIVATION WHICH CHALLENGES

Verse 11 begins with the 'fear of the Lord'. This is no synonym for basic piety, nor the quiet godliness seen in Proverbs as 'the beginning of wisdom', nor does it deny the truth of 1 John 4:18 which speaks of perfect love casting out fear. In this context, it is actually linked with the awe of final judgement. Christians do not fear the judgement to come, because through Christ's act of love on the cross we are accepted. However, in the light of judgement day, we should be given great courage not to fear those forces or people whose power is limited. Fear of the Lord should destroy fear of man.

Paul's response to the reality of the judgement seat of Christ, both for himself and his readers, was to dedicate himself to 'persuade' people (v11). The verb indicates a ministry primarily to minds and then to wills in response. All too often the theme of final judgement and the awesomeness of hell have been linked with emotional manipulation. In our society there will not be the frightening power of this message as there was in the days of the Wesleys. All the more reason, therefore, to expound the clear teaching of Scripture on this theme to inform minds not normally easily receptive to it. Not least Christians need to be persuaded of its truth to galvanise them to sacrificial and often unpopular actions and words

Ministry of reconciliation

- *Brainstorm some of the attitudes and values of the post-modern generation.*

- *In the light of these attitudes and values, what are the best tools/methods to 'persuade' people of the truth of the gospel in our generation? How well is your church doing in this area?*

Fear is never the sole Christian motivation. In verse 14 we are challenged by the love of Christ. The stress is on his love for us, not vice-versa. Too often our over-subjective modern choruses keep on announcing how great our love for Jesus is. I am always happier with the more objective songs, because I cannot doubt the reality of Christ's love and yet find it hard to know a yardstick of my love for him. For Paul the ultimate yardstick of Christ's love is the cross (see Rom. 5:8). Here as ever we are not directed to the story of Jesus and his care for the needy or his welcome of the outcast, important though that may be. We are taken straight to Calvary – 'because we are convinced that one died for all'.

Some years ago I stood by an empty cot seeking to minister to a Christian couple who had just lost a young baby. It was difficult to speak of God's love in those harrowing moments without being trite and callous. I could only go back to the cross and remind them that there was an abiding truth by which we can be sure of God's love in Christ. Present tragedies may not make sense to our finite eyes but must be interpreted in the light of the historic truth of the Calvary event. Here was the willing death of God's Son for our sake.

In verse 14 there is a lovely blend of objective truth and subjective response. It speaks of being convinced that one died for all and therefore being compelled by the truth of that measure of sacrificial love. The word translated 'compels' is used elsewhere in the New Testament of the

58 *Rhythm of the Gospel*

crowds pushing Jesus (Lk. 8:45), of the armies of Rome surrounding Jerusalem (Lk. 19:43), and of Paul's own turmoil, being torn in his decision-making (Phil. 1:23). The truth of the cross should always move us to action.

One of my most memorable experiences of this fact was a visit to our Sheffield church by the late Bishop Stephen Neill; even then a venerable missionary leader, author, expert in world religions, gracious but firmly committed to the uniqueness of the Christian gospel. After a deeply intellectually satisfying account of the message of the cross the bishop recited by memory a poem on the theme and, as he did so, tears flowed down his cheeks. Here was a profound theologian who had not lost the heart to be moved by this central truth of the faith. Yet there was much more than emotion in his response to the cross. The same message had taken him to the ends of the earth in evangelistic enterprise. How like the apostle Paul he was! He never forgot that the 'Son of God loved me and gave himself for me' (Gal. 2:20).

'Therefore all died' at the end of verse 14 is no simplistic truth but links irrevocably with the theme of Christ's death for all. In Romans chapter 6 Paul will expound that truth in more detail. It is a vivid reminder that we are all guilty as sinners for the death of Christ. With that conviction Peter, on the day of Pentecost, would indict his large crowd of hearers by telling them, 'you put him to death by nailing him to the cross' (Acts 2:23). That was not literally true of one single person in the audience and probably large numbers would never even have been guilty of crying 'Crucify' on that first Good Friday. He was, however, absolutely right spiritually and one could give the same accusation today. Yet there is a great gospel hope in the phrase 'therefore all died.' His death was, in the deepest sense, our death and his resurrection ours also. Such a truth should call for constant awesome praise and motivate us

Ministry of reconciliation 59

for dedicated service. We take up our cross, moved by the love shown in the greatest act of love in all history.

● *Explain what is meant in verse 14 that 'one died for all and therefore all died'.*

THE MINISTRY WHICH TRANSFORMS

The key to this passage is in verse 17, with Paul's dramatic claim to be 'a new creation'. In Christ there is a revolution. Rebirth does not change our temperament, at least not immediately, but it transforms our attitudes and priorities. So in the dramatic dialogue of John 3, Jesus had told the seeking Nicodemus, with all his Pharisaic hang-ups, that he needed to be born from above. The searching counter-question from the religious teacher about going back into his mother's womb was met by a clear statement that we are dealing with spiritual, not physical, qualities. In modern terms there is no call for a 're-birthing' experience but the offer of new life in the Spirit through faith in Jesus.

Some clear tests will follow. In the first place there will be a new attitude to others (v16). Paul becomes a little complex here, partly because he is writing in the context of specific false teaching and accusations. On the one hand, he wants to demonstrate that in this new creation life he cares little about the opinion of others. His whole aim is to please God; his whole ministry is exercised in the sight of God. His opponents may claim that he is out of his mind (v13) but after all they made similar aspersions about Jesus. In the eyes of the world's philosophies, there is always an apparent madness about the claims of the Christian faith – the virgin birth, the resurrection, and world history changed by a man on a gibbet. At the same time Paul wants to give ammunition to faithful souls standing up to the specious attacks of the false apostles. He seeks to

60 *Rhythm of the Gospel*

demonstrate his integrity so that others can take genuine pride in him (v12). This constitutes a particular challenge to Christian leaders in every generation. We cannot avoid the role-model scenario and therefore must live responsibly. Jesus speaks solemn words about those whose life or teaching becomes a stumbling block to young believers.

Secondly, those who are 'new creations' have a new attitude to life itself. 'Should no longer live for themselves' is the pregnant phrase in verse 15. Such an attitude is clearly contrary to the behaviour of Adam and Eve in the Garden of Eden. They disobeyed a clear command from God, and were tempted to believe that in this act of rebellion they would become like God. This sin was absolute folly and the continuance of this attitude has spoiled the created order and ruined our relationship with our Creator. Jesus, the second Adam, turned this sinful order upside down again. Here we are challenged to follow Christ's way, inspired by his Calvary act of love.

Often this new attitude to life is seen in very practical terms, such as our use of time and money. Consecration to God is seen more in what we do with our chequebooks than what we do with our hymn books. A biographer of the Duke of Wellington of Waterloo fame found him a hard man to understand until he discovered his account books. He commented that when he knew what Wellington did with his money, he knew the man. Every Christian needs constantly to look at his love in these practical ways. Money always talks! 1 John 3:16-18 are verses which should haunt us with their demand for not mere words but 'with actions and in truth'.

● *Apart from our use of time and money, in what other ways can we see our new attitude to life displayed?*

Another transformation is seen in our attitude to Christ himself. There is a worldly way of looking at him (v16).

Ministry of reconciliation

Peter was guilty of this in the dramatic encounter at Caesarea Philippi. Having confessed Jesus to be the Messiah, he immediately balked at the announcement from Jesus that he was to be a crucified and risen Messiah. Our Lord's rebuke was stern as he addressed Peter as an agent of Satan seeking to divert him from the pathway to Calvary (Mk. 8:33). Almost certainly Paul, before his conversion, had shared Peter's worldly view of Jesus, based on human considerations. This does not deny the value of the study of the historic Jesus but it does remind us that the whole biblical account is seen from the vantage point of the cross. Calvary, not Bethlehem, Nazareth or Capernaum is the centre of gravity of the gospel narrative.

Nor can we confine Jesus to the pages of Scripture, even though the Christian faith is basically an historic one. Nobody would deny the historicity of Muhammed but equally nobody claims to have a living relationship with him today. So the words of verse 17 – 'if anyone is in Christ, he is a new creation' are dramatic, daring words, almost a definition of what it means to be a Christian in any age. Knowing about Jesus is one thing; knowing him personally is life-changingly different.

- *What does it mean to be 'in Christ'? Look at 2 Corinthians 5:16-21, Colossians 1:28, 2:6 9-12.*

- *Measure yourself against these tests:*
  - *Do I have a new attitude to others?*
  - *Do I have a new attitude to life, to my use of time and money?*
  - *Do I have a new attitude to Christ?*

- *Often we disappoint ourselves and others because we don't act like a 'new creation.' In what sense is it true that a Christian is a 'new creation'? Give examples from your own life where the Holy Spirit still needs to work and you still need to make an effort to be like Jesus.*

62 *Rhythm of the Gospel*

THE MESSAGE WHICH INSPIRES

Message and ministry go hand in hand, just as life and lip are two sides of the same coin. Alec Motyer, a regular Keswick speaker, coined a lovely phrase when he wrote 'Lip without life is idle gossip; life without lip is an uninterpreted parable.' The first statement is crystal clear and much harm has been done to the cause of the gospel by thoughtless, glib, pious words that are not accompanied by consistent living. However, the second half of the adage is equally challenging. All too often we prefer to witness by our lives, lacking the courage to speak up about our faith. Such silent witness may bring words of approbation to us but it can hardly commend Jesus if his name is not on our lips. In our age of biblical illiteracy this is doubly so. Certainly silent witness has no place in Paul's concept of mission and ministry. The rhythm needs worthy living and bold speaking.

Verses 18-21 include deep theological truths that need spelling out. In verses 18-19 there is a message of reconciliation and in the beautifully phrased verse 21 there is a message of substitution. Both themes are God-centred and cross-centred. This letter makes much of the activity of God the Father. He takes the initiative in the plan of salvation (see 1:21, 4:6 and 5:5). We must never misrepresent the work of the Godhead by thinking of the Son wringing salvation from a somewhat reluctant Father. Calvary was God very much at work in a costly, united act of family sacrifice. A little child, seeing a depiction of the cross, made the understandable but misguided comment: 'If God had been there he would not have let them do it, would he?' The adult Christian should know better.

Reconciliation is an urgent issue at all times, within families, within churches, between nations and races. Scripture insists that before the horizontal relationships

Ministry of reconciliation 63

can be restored there is a basic relationship that has been marred by sin. Ever since the fall of man recounted in the early chapters of Genesis, there has been a separation between men and women on the one hand and the holy God on the other. The divine plan to restore that vertical relationship necessitated the death of the perfect God-man Jesus as our representative, our substitute. The pictures run through the pages of the Bible preparing for the world-shaking event of Calvary. There was the Passover lamb killed instead of the first born in Israelite families and still remembered in an annual celebration. Similarly there was the vivid story of the ram found in the bush that was killed as a substitute instead of Abraham's son, Isaac.

Behind the bald terms of the glorious exchange of verse 21 lies an act of deep love on the part of God, Father and Son. Such a sacrifice was only made because there was no other way for the wrath of a holy God to be satisfied. For Paul, who had to wrestle with the thought of the Messiah becoming a curse so that we should not be cursed (Gal. 3:13), there was a double challenge he could not escape. He had first to humble himself and accept this gift of salvation, sinking all his religious pride and then he had to follow the example of Jesus in self-giving service, depicted here as an ambassador with terms of peace (v20).

● *In twos, explain 2 Corinthians 5:21 as if you were talking to a non-Christian. Brainstorm helpful ways to explain 'sin' and 'righteousness of God'.*

Anyone who has sought to bring unreconciled parties together will know that someone has to take the initiative and risk being hurt, offering the right hand of forgiveness and acceptance. Yet there can be no genuine reconciliation until and unless the other party will receive the offer. It is symbolised in the service of Holy Communion. We break the bread and pour the wine, dramatic reminders of Jesus'

Rhythm of the Gospel

64

body being broken on the cross and his life-blood outpoured. Then each participant, all equal at the foot of the cross, holds out an empty hand to receive. Each time we do this we re-enact the wonder of our conversion. There are dangers in too frequent services of communion, making things glorious become stale, but at the same time the message of the cross is one we need to hear constantly.

With that in mind, Paul urgently implores people to accept the Lord's offer of reconciliation with God because of the great act of substitution by God (vv20-21). It comes as a heartfelt appeal. I have been privileged to be closely involved with the ministry of Billy Graham in this country and been moved at the sight of thousands of all ages responding to the open evangelistic appeal. There can be dangers of over-emotionalism, of crowd pressure, of too great a stress on the act of a moment. On the other hand, there is the real value of an opportunity to stand up and be counted, counselled and commissioned back to the church. Occasionally at the Keswick Convention and regularly at its worldview service we follow a similar pattern. However the word 'appeal' has a wider content. Constantly the church should be appealing for a response from the congregation. Every sermon, as in the New Testament, should demand a verdict as well as present truth. Increasingly in our post-Christian society people come to faith gradually and mostly within the orbit of the worshipping community. However we need never apologise for the appeal. Indeed this sense of urgency should be at the heart of all of us. Not surprisingly the next chapter begins with the note of 'now' and 'today'.

An Old Testament story in 2 Kings 7 underlines the great gospel truths of 2 Corinthians 5. It is the dramatic story of four leprous men expelled outside the walls of Samaria. A siege of the city ensued with no food inside or outside the city. So the men decided they had nothing to

Ministry of reconciliation

lose and in their desperation, went to the enemy camp, found it miraculously deserted with food left behind, and began to catch up on their feeding. Then conscience struck as they thought of the thousands in the city starving needlessly with a ghost enemy holding them in thrall. 'We're not doing right. This is a day of good news and we are keeping it to ourselves.' This was their caring response. For Christians in our age to keep quiet as we enjoy the blessings of the gospel is a guilty silence. For the sake of Jesus and for the sake of others, we need a new motivation to awaken us and open our mouths.

- *Like Paul, we are Christ's ambassadors entrusted with the ministry of reconciliation. What are the struggles you have carrying out this ministry? How could you improve?*
- *What warnings are there for us in Paul's message? Remember he was writing this gospel appeal of reconciliation to God to a group of Christians in an established church.*

FURTHER STUDY

Read back over the chapters you have studied so far (2 Cor. 2:14-5:21). From Paul's arguments, what do you think the false teachers in Corinth must have been saying?

Look up 'Fearing the Lord/Fear of the Lord' in a concordance. What can we learn about this concept? Look particularly at how it affects people's attitudes and behaviour towards others.

REFLECTION AND RESPONSE

Think about the different aspects of reconciliation discussed in this passage:

- Have you been reconciled to God for the first time and become a 'new creation'?

66 *Rhythm of the Gospel*

- Do you need to ask God's forgiveness for a particular sin so that you can restore your relationship with him?

- Do you need to be reconciled with another Christian?

- Do you need to be more active in offering the gospel message of reconciliation to the people you meet?

If it is appropriate, spend time in twos discussing what God has taught you from this passage and the action you need to take. Pray for each other and the particular opportunities God has given you to exercise the ministry of reconciliation.

REVIEW OF 2 CORINTHIANS 5:1-21

Chapter 5 is full of contrasts – our earthly and heavenly bodies, our status and ministry before and after our conversion. Go through the chapter picking out as many examples as possible of contrasts. Is there anything that particularly strikes you?

Amongst all these contrasts Paul's role is one of reconciliation. As believers we share Paul's role as Christ's ambassadors. How could you be a better ambassador? What new values, priorities and attitudes are important for this role? Think through what it means to be an ambassador in

- Your home
- Your workplace
- Your neighbourhood

POINTS TO PONDER

- What have you learnt about God?
- What have you learnt about yourself?
- What actions or attitudes do you need to change as a result?

CHAPTER 7

Gospel appeal

Aim: To examine our response and commendation of the gospel appeal

---

FOCUS ON THE THEME
Can you remember what first made the gospel appeal to you? Was it the attractiveness of someone's character, a certain element of the good news message, or the welcome of a congregation? How does this affect how you present and live out the gospel now?

Read: 2 Corinthians 6:1-13

The word 'ambassador' sounds dignified and our concept is of a gentleman in smart clothing representing his country on honorific occasions. But the image in the back of Paul's mind as he was writing 2 Corinthians 5:20 was of a Roman official taking terms of peace to warring tribes. Paul saw himself as taking the terms of peace to those who were warring against God. Elsewhere the apostle is more dramatic as he speaks of himself as an 'ambassador in chains' (Eph. 6:20). Paul's gospel ministry was not often one of being lauded on a platform; he was usually in prison or defending himself against misrepresentation. And in chapter 6:1-13 he demonstrates how costly gospel ministry can be as he opens his heart to the Corinthians. Paul has often had a bad press as a hard man or one who

68 *Rhythm of the Gospel*

made the simple teaching of Jesus demanding and difficult. Nothing could be further from the truth; his ambassadorship made him very vulnerable.

I have often used the opening verses of this chapter when speaking to Christians prior to evangelistic missions that I have led throughout the United Kingdom. They drive home the need to act now and not at some vague distant date when it might be easier and more convenient. There is no time like the present for outreach. Yet appeals must come with gentle persuasiveness, not with ferocity of tone. I was taught the noble game of cricket when a bowler's appeal was meant to be a sincere questioning of the umpire. Now 'owzat' is shrieked at the poor official with a fist under his nose, hoping that he'll change his decision and jerk his finger heavenwards. A true Christian appeal should always be with grace.

AN URGENT APPEAL

It is to fellow-believers that Paul writes with the exhortation not to receive God's grace in vain (6:1). He himself was never complacent, fearing that having preached to others he might be found to have wasted a life (1 Cor. 9:27). The gospel message and subsequent experience of God in our lives are not merely for our eternal satisfaction. They bring a solemn responsibility to pass on the good news to others. This is all part of the rhythm of the gospel. The picture is akin to the Olympic runners carrying the torch from Mount Olympus until it burns above the latest expensive venue for the Games. In that task there is a certain loneliness but also the joy of being 'fellow-workers'.

● *Share examples of how Christians can receive God's grace 'in vain' (v1)?*

Gospel appeal

What greater privilege can there be than working alongside God, being his fellow-workers? The Lord Jesus commissioned the first disciples to go and make disciples, ending with the promise that he would always be with them as they launched out into this impossible enterprise (Mt. 28:19-20). The history of the church proves how well those pioneers succeeded and we should take heart accordingly. The term 'fellow-workers' contains the note of team ministry. From the beginning witness was meant to be a communal activity. Jesus sent his disciples out two by two; on the day of Pentecost Peter stood with the eleven as he preached the first church sermon in the open air. Often we fail to discover true Christian unity because we are always talking about it. Engagement in mission brings us together and makes some of the hot debating issues merely peripheral. In my lifetime the arrival of evangelist Dr Billy Graham to a city has brought denominations and differing schools of thought into a united enterprise to preach the fundamentals of the faith. Sadly, experience teaches that fairly soon after the event we dash back to our comfortable ghettos and undo much of the good that has been done.

● *What does it mean to you to be one of God's 'fellow workers'?*

One remedy to our ghetto mentality is to be reminded of the dangers of a delayed response to the evangelistic challenge. Years ago I was discovered hiding behind a convenient phrase. Whenever my wife reminded me of some domestic matter calling for my attention, I would almost without thinking offer to do something about it 'one of these days'. One of those days I found pinned to my desk a list of the jobs I had promised to do 'one of these days' with an extra column headed ' Date done'. The medicine worked. Never again did I use that phrase, at least not in my wife's hearing. How often do we say 'one

Rhythm of the Gospel

of these days' when listening to and talking with the Lord? Jesus told a brief parable about two sons (Mt. 21:28-32). One refused to obey his father but then had a change of heart; the other promised glibly, 'I will, sir' but the Scripture pertinently adds 'but he did not go'. That parable is often re-enacted in the lives of Christians.

So Paul puts the word 'now 'at the heart of the equation in 2 Corinthians 6:2. He is quoting the prophet Isaiah speaking about the hour of grace in which we now live, as Jesus did in his synagogue sermon in his hometown of Nazareth (Lk. 4:18-21). There are occasions where the servant of God has to wait for the right time for action. Moses had forty years' apprenticeship before God deemed him ready and the newly converted Paul spent three years in the Arabian desert before he began public ministry. We can be in too much of a hurry sometimes. Yet the reverse is equally true. The wealthy tax collector Zaccheus, eager to glimpse Jesus from the vantage point of a tree, was challenged to come down and welcome the preacher into his home 'today'. Propriety would have suggested a private encounter at some convenient time in the future but Jesus was on his way to Jerusalem and the cross; he would never pass that way again. It literally was now or never. We are not in charge of our futures and must beware of the danger of a delayed response to the call to commitment and service. In many lives there is a tragic 'if only', bringing the sadness of contemplating what might have been.

A CONSISTENT APPEAL

It is possible to be a negative witness. We can make it harder for people to come to faith. People will always find excuses for not believing. But it is tragic when the lives of believers provide the excuse. Paul himself feared he might become a

Gospel appeal

stumbling block (6:3) – hence verses 4-13 detailing his life of service and its demands. It sounds like self-commendation but it is actually a resumé of the cost of following Jesus. This is no ego trip but the story of a man devoted to following the footsteps of his Master. Ironically it is when the church has been at its most demanding that it has achieved its greatest success. Ease and popularity quickly stifle the Spirit.

● *In your own context what are the 'stumbling blocks' for believers?*

This autobiographical sketch is all about service and the word 'deacon', which the NIV translates as 'servant' in verse 4, is at its heart. It is a word lifted to great heights by the dramatic example of Jesus in John 13 when he took the towel and performed the job of a slave, significantly at a moment when the disciples had been arguing about status. All too rarely has the church lived up to this standard. Hierarchical structures fit ill with the New Testament teaching and the way of Jesus. Perhaps we shall only make an impact again when they see the towel symbol at the heart of church life and especially Christian leadership

Sacrifice not popularity is at the heart of verses 4-5 with a catalogue, repeated in chapter 11, of painful experiences in the cause of gospel ministry. The hunger mentioned in verse 5 was not a period of fasting because of his religious zeal but the cost of missionary service and arduous travel. With the prosperity gospel of our contemporary church and the even more prevalent middle class comfortable ghetto life, we are light years away from Paul's experience. We need to remember that the Bible does not promise success at every turn and much harm has been done by offering a crossless discipleship. Jesus was always realistic and told his disciples that following him would bring joy and ultimately resurrection life and yet the pathway would be strewn with thorns as well as roses.

Rhythm of the Gospel

● *Clearly we don't share Paul's list of hardships so how do we 'commend ourselves' to Christians and non-Christians?*

We need to keep a balanced perspective on the Christian life. Christianity is not world-denying nor is it hair shirt asceticism and it does offer abundant life (Jn. 10:10). There are promises of healing, even if the signs and wonders of the Gospels are a unique testimony to the ministry of Jesus and under-gird his claims. However it is not possible in the light of those promises to assume that health is always our right. Occasionally dramatic stories of supposed divine intervention in matters of health and healing create a crisis in our view of the nature of God. For Paul the badge of faithful discipleship was not glorious experiences but endurance under pressure.

In verse 4 in this list of suffering for the gospel, the word the NIV translates as 'distress' can also be translated 'narrow places'. There is a vivid illustration in the story of the Exodus. Newly out of Egypt and being pursued by the army of Pharaoh, the children of Israel are told to stand still and see God's salvation (Ex. 14:13). This was a truly narrow place with the sea in front, the army behind, the mountains on one side and the desert on the other. We talk today about being between a rock and a hard place! Here was the perfect example and yet soon an act of God happened which became, in Scripture, the prototype for the work of salvation through cross and resurrection. God has his purpose in the narrow places and Paul was often there.

Costly service produces the right kind of spirituality. In verse 6 the 'holy spirit' comes in the middle of a list of Christian virtues bred in the world of godly testing. Probably the phrase should not have capital letters and refers to the individual spirit of holiness rather than the third person of the Trinity. However, it is only through the Holy Spirit that these qualities of kindness, love and patience can be created in us. The reality of these spiritual

Gospel appeal

73

qualities is often reflected by the words we speak. Jesus speaks of us being judged by our words and his brother James, reflecting this teaching, has much to say about the power of the tongue for good or ill in his own letter. It is not surprising, therefore, that when the prophet Isaiah records his dramatic call to service, he remembers vividly confessing the sins of his 'unclean lips' and being cleansed by the burning coals (Is. 6:5-7). So here in verse 7 Paul sees truthful speech as a powerful weapon, just as Hebrews 4:12 speaks of the Word of God as a double-edged sword.

● *Look at the ways Paul commends the gospel (vv4-10). Is God challenging you to commend the gospel in any of the specific ways he called Paul to do? What steps do you need to take to make this a reality?*

This letter has always to be seen and understood in the context of the false teachers with whom the apostle was in conflict. They were often specious, charismatic figures painting a very attractive picture and in contrast Paul seemed an old-fashioned spoilsport. Knowing we would face similar dilemmas, Jesus warned us to watch out for the false prophets who look good but must be judged by their words (Mt. 7:15-20). Those who speak the truth must also seek to be gracious and genuinely attractive but we must be alert to the 'nice man' scenario. Often the purveyors of heresy have a good media personality and lead the unsuspecting astray. In Paul's book, the real test of the divine stamp upon a ministry is the power of the truth to change lives (1 Thes. 1:5).

Truth is not always popular and those who seek general approval for their ministries will shy away from the message that brings opposition more than applause. Verses 8-10 in poetic form encapsulates a lifetime of costly sacrifice. Paul believes that this way of suffering commends him as a faithful follower of the true Suffering

74   *Rhythm of the Gospel*

Servant. It was not all gloom and doom. Paul had great joy in seeing individuals come to faith and churches founded. The paradox is repeated in these verses in different contrasts. Like his Master, he could have avoided much of the suffering but in so doing, he would have missed out on the blessings. This is poignantly expressed in the final words 'poor yet making many rich; having nothing yet possessing everything' (6:10). The Pharisee turned Christian preacher went into a life of material poverty and social exclusion but knew the unique riches of Christian fellowship across race and class and the assurance of the eternal reward of seeing people saved from hell and now in the glory of heaven.

- *Many of us feel inadequate and not able to say 'as servants of God we commend ourselves in every way'. Look back over the chapters you have studied – does Paul say anything to give you confidence and encouragement?*
- *How would you respond to someone who claimed that in these verses Paul was taking pride in his hardships?*

A COMPASSIONATE APPEAL

Every preacher knows something of the pathos of verses 11-13. Here is a pastor pouring out his heart, for a true preacher will always have a pastor's heart. Paul was following in the steps of Jesus who wept over Jerusalem and cried 'How often have I longed to gather your children together as a hen gathers her chicks under her wings, but you were not willing' (Mt. 23:37). Not even Jesus could force a response from the people he loved. Love always makes a person vulnerable, for love can only plead and try to persuade; it cannot force. This truth may lie behind the mystery of the creation of man. Clearly Almighty God

Gospel appeal 75

could have created robotic beings to obey him like Dr Who's Daleks. Such creatures could never have responded in love. Men and women made 'in the image of God' can respond to God and have a unique relationship with him. And in that relationship we see the heart of God who weeps over those he has made, who still reject his overtures of love. So elsewhere, writing of his relationship with his fellow Israelites, Paul was willing to be cursed by God if by so doing he could win them for Christ. But such a transfer would be quite impossible (Rom. 9:1-3).

Paul is not only a preacher-pastor: he sees himself as the father of the Corinthian believers, since he was the pioneer whose ministry brought them to new birth in the spiritual sense (1 Cor. 4:15). In verse 13, he calls the Corinthians his 'children'. In some churches, the title of 'Father' is used. Many of us would fight shy of such names but the spirit behind the title is right. Indeed, in many broken homes, it may be the only way to rescue the 'Father' title and enable people to see, dimly but truly, the character of God the Father. His loving affection is also seen in the personal reference to his readers by name – 'Corinthians' in verse 11. This unusual way of referring to his reader is seen in Galatians 3:1. His love of these Galatians, despite their backsliding, is evident. Similarly, in Philippians 4:15 he mentions the Philippians by name, in joyful acknowledgement of their generosity.

● *'If you open your heart to the gospel you must open your heart to others who believe it.' In what ways do you particularly struggle with this?*

In this loving affectionate openness Paul is not denying his apostolic authority and soon he will revert to the challenge of ' no compromise.' But in these verses Paul is asking them to play fair. He is being open with the Corinthian believers, sharing his thoughts and concerns.

Rhythm of the Gospel

All too often they are holding back. Openness or speaking freely has its problems. It can be a cover for rudeness. I have learned to steer clear of the so-called friend who assures me that he is speaking the truth in love. The truth may be more obvious than the love! Yet we must work at speaking truthfully since in a world of diplomacy and spin, the first casualty is an open spirit. Here is one of the great values of small groups in the life of a church, where individuals know each other well enough to open up on the most intimate of subjects, knowing that there will be both loving, prayerful understanding and a confidentiality to be trusted. The gossip, and churches easily breed them, will always undermine that pastoral sensitivity shown by Paul and coveted by every genuine believer.

- *In a small group situation, how can you establish trust so that people are willing to 'open wide' their hearts?*

- *How should we react if despite being open and affectionate towards other Christians, they continue to rebuff us? Are there Bible verses that help you deal with this issue?*

- *Put yourself in the following scenarios: how should you 'speak the truth in love'?*

  - *Someone has volunteered to play the piano in the church music group. They are not particularly talented but very enthusiastic. They come to all the practices but are not really up to the standard of the rest of the musicians. How will you deal with this sensitive situation?*

  - *A child is particularly disruptive in junior church and vying for attention. His parents are Christians but have only recently started coming to your church. Would you speak to them about the child? What would you say?*

  - *Someone has misconstrued your behaviour towards them but instead of talking to you about it they broke down in tears in the home group and told all the people there. You heard about this incident second-hand. What should you do now?*

FURTHER STUDY

Paul says in verse 2 that 'now is the time of God's favour, now is the day of salvation'. Many centuries earlier Isaiah and the Psalmist claimed the same – see Isaiah 49:8, 55:6, Psalm 69:13. How can both be true?

REFLECTION AND RESPONSE

Take time to reflect on these verses individually. Perhaps you are going through a particular difficulty like Paul and need to ask for God's strength. You may need to repent for receiving God's grace in vain. You may want to bring your life and ministry to God and pray that he will use it to commend the gospel.

Then, in twos or threes, spend time 'opening wide your hearts' to each other. Share what's going on in your life and specific ways the other group members can pray for you or provide practical support.

CHAPTER 8

No compromise

Aim: To renew our commitment to holiness

FOCUS ON THE THEME
Spend five minutes drafting a rough timetable of your typical week. Where do you spend most of your time? Where do you have to make compromises? To what extent does how you spend your time reflect your true commitments and priorities? Apart from time with God, how else do you demonstrate your commitment to holiness?

Read: 2 Corinthians 6:14–7:1

As a preacher I find that certain texts of Scripture bring back memories – of all kinds! 2 Corinthians 7:1 takes me back to a Sunday morning in St Thomas' Edinburgh. In the congregation was Dr Alan Redpath. Recently retired from a powerful pastorate at Charlotte Baptist Chapel, he was between ministries. He and I were to become firm friends and colleagues in Christian service, not least at the Keswick Convention. Then, however, I was a nervous young man with a well-known preacher in the back pew. I had preached this passage in 2 Corinthians and after the service Alan was kind enough to comment on the sermon with the prediction that I would one day join him on the Keswick platform and then I should resurrect this sermon as very applicable for such a moment. I was suitably

No compromise

honoured, the prediction became true, but I never did preach on the text.

Some scholars suggest that 6:14-7:1 are a late insertion from some other piece of writing. Certainly 6:11-13 moves very naturally into 7:2-4 with its note of warm, open-hearted ministry. On the other hand it is equally possible that Paul, with an inspired butterfly mind, jumps quickly from the thought of fatherhood in 6:13 to the danger of misinterpreting that as a soft option. The fatherhood of God must be treated with awe and respect. When Jesus prayed to his Father he called him 'holy Father'. Within a loving relationship, there is the note of jealousy and exclusivism. So Paul will urge these Christians not to indulge in two-timing with a holy father God.

Such devotion to God is costly. Jesus never under-estimated the cost of following him. Luke 9:57-62 records the account of a trio of would-be followers whom Jesus challenged to give him absolute and immediate priority, if they were serious. The conditions for service haven't changed. God still calls us to take up our cross and follow. In Old Testament days Gideon had to whittle down his army to the utterly dedicated three hundred before God would give the victory. Ironically it is often the Christian fellowship that keeps the standards high which draws a committed group of young people to its cause. Recently a local journalist was visiting a church. He expressed his surprise that a place that dared to speak out against unbiblical sexual practice attracted such a crowd of teenagers and students. The vicar pointed out to the sceptical media man that it was precisely because of its stance, not in spite of it, that young people came back week after week.

Paul elsewhere uses the analogy of the soldier, athlete and farmer (2 Tim. 2) as examples of single-minded devotion to the task in hand. There is no room for the dilettante Christian in the Lord's service. An obituary in a

Rhythm of the Gospel

newspaper said of a deceased lady that, 'religion was her chief hobby'. Happily she was not alive to read such a travesty of the truth. Yet this is no call to some monastic disappearance from the real world. Rather it is a call to live out this dedication in the world, showing our different priorities. The great pioneers of faith in the book of Genesis pitched their tents and built their altars. They were busy and successful men in society but worldly possessions were seen as transitory; it was the spiritual element that was important and eternal. Our modern society has all the hallmarks of the wicked city of Corinth and like those first believers, we are called to live lives of no compromise, with the right motivation and towards godly sanctification.

CHRISTIAN MOTIVATION

In 7:1 the word 'these' is emphatic. There are plenty of promises in Scripture to encourage and even make the mouth water in anticipation (see 2 Pet. 1:4 for example). The closing verses of chapter 6 are quite enough to motivate us to a life of no compromise in our relationship with God and with the world. Not least is the staggering truth of verse 16 that 'we are the temple of the living God'. For a practising Jew like Paul with his great respect for the Jerusalem temple in all its glory, this is a call for holiness of life in every aspect. The Old Testament with its detailed account of the building of the temple and the prophet Ezekiel with his vision of a temple in the restored Jerusalem, make it clear how God demands perfect purity in every part – priest and building alike. Here is the divine visual aid for the life of the believer.

- *Brainstorm what it means to be 'holy'.*
- *Can you think of a more modern visual aid to emphasise the purity and holiness that God requires?*

No compromise 81

This temple analogy is both individual and corporate. In 1 Corinthians 6:19 it speaks of the Christian's body as the Spirit's temple; in 1 Corinthians 3:16 the church is that temple. Both must be held together with the double challenge that my life and the community to which I belong in Christ should reflect God's holiness. So in the book of Nehemiah the scoundrel Tobiah was kicked out from his illegitimate residence in the temple. In the Acts swift judgement came upon Ananias and Sapphira for their sin of lying to God and despising his Spirit. I often meet enthusiastic Christians who long for a return to the miraculous activities of the early church but are horrified when I enquire whether the judgement miracle of Acts 5 is in their programme. We can be so gloriously selective in our reading of the Bible! The sudden death of Ananias and his wife was a solemn reminder of the purity and holiness that God demands.

The New Testament takes the body seriously (7:1). Unlike some spiritualities and many old religions, Christianity is not some soul-based activity which makes no demands upon how we treat our body. In 1 Corinthians 6 and its temple reference, the body is seen as important because of creation, redemption, the indwelling of the Spirit, and the hope of resurrection. The injunction 'therefore honour God in your body' is the natural and demanding corollary. What we see; how we work; our sexual activity and principles; health and priorities seen in our use of time and money – all these are 'temple' issues as we rejoice in God's promise.

In verse 16 God gives a more intimate promise as he promises to live with his people in a reciprocal bond. These words had been uttered at Mount Sinai when God made special vows to his chosen people and they responded appropriately. There is a kind of marriage analogy here. In preparing couples for marriage in church

82 *Rhythm of the Gospel*

I would often demonstrate the gospel overtones of the wedding service. For example, the 1662 Book of Common Prayer directs couples to loose hands after the bridegroom has made his vows. Then the same hands return to their loving grasp as a symbol that the bride is in no forced liaison. Of her own free will she enacts her commitment. So it is with the people of God and their bridegroom the Lord. He takes the initiative and makes the offer; we respond in an act of loving obedience. It is not without significance that the last occurrence of this particular promise is in Revelation 21:3 on the day of the bridal feast of the Lamb. Then the relationship will be fully consummated and eternally enjoyed; until then we rejoice at his promise and remember our vows.

Paul rings the changes in his metaphors and goes back in verse 18 to 2 Samuel 7:14 where God promised Solomon a father-son relationship. This has dynamic implications for those who follow Jesus, who encouraged us to call the sovereign God and his eternal father 'our Father'. The temple building may have stood in Jerusalem as a symbolic reminder of God's presence with his people, just as the church spire seeks to bring us back to our heritage. Buildings, however, can be dangerous, leading to false confidence in institutions rather than the truth and the God they represent. No wonder Jesus had to cleanse the temple at the beginning and end of his ministry.

● *In these verses Paul relays God's promise to live among us and to be our father. To what extent were these promises conditional in the Old Testament: to what extent are they conditional upon our holiness now?*

Our key verse, 7:1, not only reminds us that motivation springs from the promises of God but also from the purity of God. The phrase here is 'out of reverence for God'. The note is of fear, a desire not to displease the God who has

No compromise

saved and called us. Paul is echoing the language of Leviticus 19:2 with its command to ' be holy because I the Lord your God am holy'. Often we dismiss the book of Leviticus as being so remote and of a different culture that it is utterly meaningless today. In fact, the call to holiness is very practical and contemporary. In the rest of chapter 19 we are challenged to care about the environment; to pay just wages; to consider the poor; to avoid the occult; to keep the Sabbath; to care about blind and deaf; to show respect for the elderly That would make a splendid manifesto for any contemporary political party.

● *Be honest. What motivates you to perfect your holiness? On a scale of 1-10 (1 being not at all and 10 being extremely important) how great a motivation is 'reverence for God'?*

In every age this holy way of life will be in marked contrast with prevailing society. So in verse 17 Paul quotes words from Isaiah, with its reference to the return from exile, and demands a coming out, a separation. Almost since the days of the Wesleys over two hundred years ago, there has been a level of agreed Christian morality in the normally accepted patterns of behaviour. That has now virtually disappeared and the call for a counter-culture must be heard and its implications faced. We are back in Corinthian days. Like the exiles we need a separation, a coming out.

This challenge lies behind the language of verse 14 and the danger of the double harness. For generations this has been the proof text in matters of marriage and the danger of intimate relationships with non-Christians. There is no doubt about the relevance here. How many Christians have abandoned their faith because of marriages with non-Christians? True unity can hardly be found where there is disagreement in the most fundamental area. The affairs of

84 *Rhythm of the Gospel*

the heart inevitably create tensions and I have had few more painful pastoral situations than having to intervene in potential mismatches. The principle, however, has many manifestations. A well-known Christian businessman testified that he was saved from an unhelpful joint business enterprise by an apparent throwaway line in a Keswick address on this theme.

● *A young person from the church youth group challenges you about your view that Christians should not marry unbelievers. They say that the passage in 2 Corinthians 6 is talking about false teachers not personal relationships. How would you respond? Are there other passages you could point them to in order to portray the biblical view of marriage?*

There is a string of opposites in verse 14, clear black and white. Righteousness is contrasted with wickedness; light with darkness; Christ with Satan; the believer with the unbeliever. Yet as we seek to show forth the purity of God, the light of Christ, we live in a world of shades of grey. Someone put the challenge in a useful aphorism, 'In things essential, purity; in things non-essential, unity; in all things, charity.' This is a valuable rule of thumb inside the church, where all too often we fight over secondary issues and spoil unity over trivia. It is also an important guideline for our relationships with those in the world.

There is one other phrase in our key text that cannot go unnoticed. In 7:1 Paul calls his readers 'dear friends' which more than softens the blow before the punchline. If you doubted this you would be convinced as you read the touching words of affection in verses 7:2-4. The apostle never fought shy of expressing his love for his converts, even when they let him down. I have always been impressed by the willingness of many of my Christian forbears to spend long years of pastoral care in isolated

No compromise 85

communities even when they were national figures in their day. The great Scottish theologian and hymn writer Samuel Rutherford cared so much for his people in rural Anwoth in the Borders that he wrote in the hymn 'The sands of time are sinking' of his deep longing to see their souls one day 'in Immanuel's land'. Years ago I visited the churchyard at Anwoth and prayed that I might have his shepherd's heart, if not his poetic skills.

● *How does calling his readers 'dear friends' demonstrate Paul's holiness? What lessons can we learn from him about dealing with people?*

CHRISTIAN SANCTIFICATION

There are many kinds of spirituality – it is the buzzword of the early twenty-first century. The New Age has a very popular spirituality fed by eastern religions and cultures: Buddhism prefers yoga, meditation and being taken out of self; within the wider Christian market many have espoused Catholic spirituality which can make the old evangelical formula of the daily quiet time, the weekly prayer meeting and Sunday worship seem old hat. But whilst there are many versions of spirituality, there is only one kind of sanctification – Christian sanctification.

Sanctification is a two-way activity. We cannot accomplish it without God and he chooses not to do it without us. 2 Corinthians 6:16-18 have already reminded us of the strength that comes from our recollection of what God has done and our relationship with him in Christ. Now in 7:1 comes the challenge to personal effort in response. 'Let us purify ourselves' is a call to come out and be different. 'Perfecting holiness' is a call to go on and become more worthy of our Christian calling, daring to follow biblical ideals and standards in an increasingly

Rhythm of the Gospel

hostile world. It is tough but never boring, spurring each other on to make a mark for God in the world.

● *Individual holiness is a very personal issue. In what practical ways we can spur each other on to be holy? What are the pitfalls to avoid?*

The Old Testament remains the perfect picture book for these New Testament truths about purity and holiness. The call in 6:17 to come out and be separate is straight from the challenge to people in exile (Is. 52:11) and that verse itself goes back to the priestly code, where every kind of detail of ablutions is found to ensure that those who touch sacred vessels have clean hands. The Christian church has no such priesthood today, following the final sacrifice of Christ our High Priest. It is sad therefore that in some denominations there is still recourse to strange rituals as if we were still in pre-Christian worship. The more urgent contemporary call is to the whole church as a priesthood of all believers to dare to be different in pure living.

The Old Testament story of Nehemiah rebuilding the Jerusalem walls is another illustration of protecting the purity of believers. The rebuilding programme was commended as a way of keeping the Jewish people separate as well as providing protection from an outside enemy. The church always has more to fear from heresy and disunity from within than from dangerous anti-Christian forces from outside. The final chapter of Nehemiah is all about a pure temple, a pure Sabbath, and a pure race. None of these has literal parallels today but the themes of the purity of the Lord's house, the Lord's day and the Lord's people are absolutely central.

Always the balance must be kept of being separate from the world and of being part of it. Zechariah 2:4 promises a new Jerusalem without walls. The book of Jonah is there as a counter-weight to Nehemiah, with its missionary call to

No compromise

care for the souls of the enemy city Nineveh. Even in chapters of the Old Testament that are full of hope of return to freedom from exile, there is the reminder to live as worthy citizens in the land of captivity. So Jeremiah chapter 29, with its glorious promises of a great future, contains verse 7 with its call to seek the peace of Babylon and to work for its prosperity. Daniel and his friends knew and obeyed this command with distinction and often at great cost. Lions and furnaces often mark the route of living for the biblical God in the world at any point in its history.

The temptation to choose the easy way is always strong, so that compromise becomes a constant danger. When in the book of Genesis, Lot parted company with Uncle Abraham and 'pitched his tent toward Sodom' he no doubt meant to live differently in that wicked city. Eventually, having failed miserably to transform the city, he had to be dragged out by the skin of his teeth before Sodom disintegrated. God had promised Abraham in Genesis 18:32 that if there were ten righteous people found in Sodom he would spare the city but even ten could not be found. Compromise in the areas of money, sex, business, language, and religion always ends the same way – disaster. The church is meant to be in the world like a boat in the sea riding the storms and rescuing some from its waves; if the world gets in the church, like the sea in the boat, there is only one direction and that is fatally downwards.

- *How far should we take Paul's teaching, 'Do not be yoked together with unbelievers'? Consider the following scenarios and explain what you would do. Discuss how Paul's teaching relates to each case.*

    - *Tom refuses to work for a non-Christian employer because he considers this being 'unequally yoked'.*

    - *Elizabeth is worried about working in a medical practice where the other GPs refer their patients for what some*

88 *Rhythm of the Gospel*

would consider to be New Age treatments. She is concerned that she might be implicitly condoning what they are doing and that others would associate her with these practices.

- *Jane's best friend is a non-Christian but she feels some pressure from church that this friendship shouldn't be such a high priority.*
- *'If the world gets in the church, like the sea in the boat, there is only one direction and that is fatally downwards.' How can we protect the purity and holiness of the church?*

If coming out in biblical separation is challenging, equally demanding is the call to go on in consistent, maturing discipleship. The phrase in verse 1 is 'perfecting holiness'. It has the note of performing religious duties but the converted Pharisee has little time for the minutiae of the law; rather he is anxious that his readers should follow Christ's way in daily living and mature in the process. The Bible does not conceive of perfection in terms of absolute freedom from sin in this world. Wrong views here have led to much folly and many casualties. It does, however, speak often of the demand to keep growing in the Christian life. Hence Jesus' words in the Sermon on the Mount 'Be perfect, therefore, as your heavenly Father is perfect' (Mt. 5:48).

Too often the New Testament notes the tragedy of falling away in the path of discipleship. Paul enquires angrily who bewitched and led astray the young Galatian Christians who had been doing so well (Gal. 3:1-5). He likens their backsliding to people running a race but tripped up by others (Gal. 5:7). The image of athletics is common in Paul's writings. Similarly, the writer to the Hebrews, with a Jewish congregation in mind who were in danger of taking the easy way of compromise, tells them to 'run with perseverance the race marked out for us' (Heb. 12:1).

No compromise

- *Identify what is contaminating your body and spirit. What is getting in the way of you growing in holiness?*

Stickability may be a dubious word but it is a vital quality in the Christian life. In his last letter of 2 Timothy, Paul laments that many have deserted him, including the previously loyal Demas 'because he loved this world.' That may be a reference to hankering after what some label 'worldliness' – the pleasures and popularity of non-Christian friends and contemporaries or simply espousing the standards of the world, giving us easy acceptance in society. Or it may simply refer to Demas making sure that he would not suffer Paul's fate in prison and his insecure future. Either way, the challenge and choice remain. The way of holy living is never likely to be popular with its demands. We need to remind ourselves constantly that we follow the Christ of Calvary who insisted that one of the marks of being a disciple was to take up our cross. That will often be painful but it is the gateway to resurrection life.

FURTHER STUDY

2 Corinthians 6:16 talks about God walking among his people. The Bible frequently talks of God and Jesus walking. Brainstorm as many examples of this as possible from both the Old and New Testaments. What lessons do you learn about God the Father and God the Son?

REFLECTION AND RESPONSE

As an individual, reflect on your answers to the questions, take time to measure your holiness. In what areas do you fall short? What is God challenging you about in particular?

As a group, re-read the passage and pick out key words or phrases from the Bible text and from the study guide. From the list each choose one word that has a particular significance to you and explain your choice to the others. For example you might list words

90 *Rhythm of the Gospel*

like 'promise', 'compromise' and 'holiness' and the word which is most significant to you now is 'promise' because at this moment in your life you are trusting God to keep a certain promise.

REVIEW OF 2 CORINTHIANS 6:1-7:1
Re-read the passage. From what Paul has written, what would you imagine his advice to be in the following scenarios? Use other passages of Scripture to help you formulate principles to deal with these issues if necessary.

- A young girl says she doesn't want to become a Christian because she has seen how badly those in and outside the church treat her father, a church minister.

- A teenage boy doesn't want to come to church any more because he thinks that his peers in the youth group are embarrassing, odd and out of touch with the real world.

- A woman feels guilty that she didn't go to the front of church to respond when the minister gave a gospel appeal. Although she prayed the prayer for salvation where she sat, she feels that she has missed out on part of the conversion experience by not going forward publicly.

POINTS TO PONDER
- What have you learnt about God?
- What have you learnt about yourself?
- What actions or attitudes do you need to change as a result?

CHAPTER 9

Ministry of encouragement

Aim: To learn how we can help ourselves and others flourish spiritually

---

FOCUS ON THE THEME
Share together examples of times you have received great encouragement and known real joy in your Christian life.
What part did sorrow or repentance play in your stories?
Which helped you grow most spiritually – the joy or the pain?

Read: 2 Corinthians 7:2-16

2 Corinthians 7:5 takes us back to 2:13 and its reference to Macedonia and Paul eagerly awaiting news from Titus. If the intervening verses have been a mere parenthesis they must be amongst the most inspired insertion in literature. We have seen the great truths of the rhythm of the gospel, the truth grasping the mind and motivating the will in constant, often sacrificial, mission and ministry. Now we are back to the human face behind the theology and the tone is one of encouragement. Titus did in fact come back with good news of the Corinthian church and as a result Paul's spirit is lifted (v13).

We may not be sure of the details related to the letter Paul had previously sent to the Corinthians (v8). But we do know that though there had been much hurt there had been some healing. Clearly the apostle had written a letter,

92 *Rhythm of the Gospel*

no longer available to us, which had hurt him as much as the recipients (see 2:4). It is part of Christian care and pastoral responsibility to dare to speak the truth even if, as with Paul, we are misunderstood and misrepresented. Most of us prefer the quiet life and the accolade of being nice men and women. But in these situations we face a choice whether to speak the truth or not. Despite the pain, the challenge of honesty often brings people to repentance and then joy. The psalmist of centuries ago speaks powerfully here as in most human situations. In Psalm 126:5-6 he comments that, 'those who sow in tears will reap with songs of joy. He who goes out weeping carrying seed to sow, will return with songs of joy carrying sheaves with him.' There is no shortcut in the spiritual life. This chapter demonstrates that the ministry of refreshment and rejoicing starts with a ministry of repentance.

● *If we have two of Paul's letters to the Corinthians in our Bibles, why do you think that we don't have this other letter?*

A MINISTRY OF REPENTANCE

The New Testament majors on the call to repentance when the good news is proclaimed. John the Baptist, Jesus himself, Peter and Paul all agreed on the necessity of a change of mind and attitude which constitutes repentance before there can be any enjoyment of the blessings of a new life. However, in Paul's letters, there is less emphasis on the challenge to believers to come to the place of repentance. These verses are an exception because as in 12:21 there is the fear that, in spite of Paul's intervention, there may be a sad lack of penitence.

What lay behind this particular call to repentance is not clear. It may have involved Paul's own authority – hence the language of verse 12. In 1 Corinthians 5 it had been a

Ministry of encouragement

matter of sexual immorality of a very serious nature and sadly there had been no disciplinary action. Indeed the church had been blasé about the whole business. These two issues are painfully contemporary. Refusal to accept biblical authority on matters of doctrine and morality has become almost the norm and compromise on issues of sexuality seems almost institutionalised. A church which could hold a celebration of homosexual relationships in a cathedral or talk in terms of sanctioning same-sex marriages is in desperate need of genuine repentance and a change of heart. It was not without wisdom that the Keswick Convention traditionally began its week of teaching with the message of sin in the life of the believer. The promised blessings of the Spirit-filled life could not be envisaged until repentance had happened. The poverty of much church life today and the haemorrhaging of young people from its midst is proof of compromise within rather than the inroads of unbelief from without.

● *To what extent is repentance part of your spiritual life? In practice how do we maintain the balance of seeing ourselves as sinners as well as those righteous in God's sight?*

● *Why is repentance the first step to spiritual growth?*

In Corinth Paul's strong medicine apparently worked. So he can speak in verses 9-11 of 'godly sorrow' and rejoice in its outworking. There is the worldly equivalent that leads to resentment, bitterness and hopelessness. Judas Iscariot and his suicide provide the illustration of the futility of worldly sorrow. In contrast you can find godly sorrow in the life of David after his heinous sin with Bathsheba, sin which embraced lying, adultery, murder and yet was the prelude to the wonderful penitential Psalm 51 where many penitent sinners have found the path to restoration (see also Ps. 32:1-5). The great story of the Prodigal Son is of the same ilk. Here Jesus teaches the truth of a Father waiting to receive

Rhythm of the Gospel

back into full son-ship the young man who acknowledged his sin and rebellion not only in word but also in humble retracing of his steps. Sometimes God allows us to fall very far before we come home. The various nouns in verse 11, 'indignation', 'alarm', 'longing', 'concern', 'readiness' are the exact opposite of the desire to excuse or justify ourselves which is the natural way of the world.

- *Look at verses 9-11. What are the behaviour and attitudes that characterise godly and worldly sorrow?*
- *How do you feel about causing someone sorrow so that they are led to repentance? What are the risks you would have to take? Can you imagine a scenario when this might happen?*

At every level we need to see this ministry of repentance at work. It will always fight against the natural tendency to explain away what the Bible calls sin or the exact opposite which is to despair individually or take vengeance on those with whom we may be in dispute. All this is seen in embryo in the early chapters of the Bible. Adam and Eve in disobedience tried to pass the buck of responsibility rather than face the consequences. Cain in envy murdered his brother Abel and pleaded that he was not his brother's keeper. Nothing in essence has changed. Into that vicious circle of sin and self-justification has, however, come the gospel of grace that alone offers a way back to God through acknowledgement of sin, true repentance and a new start. This gospel has world-changing implications.

A MINISTRY OF REFRESHMENT

There can be an unbiblical solemnity about some church services and Christian ministries. Without espousing the

Ministry of encouragement 95

froth and superficiality of the other extreme which caricatures Christian joy as maniacal laughter, silly smiling or sheer escapism, Keswick has sought to encourage the enjoyment of worship and listening to God's word. There is plenty of humour around the 'sacred tent'. Humour can be a great servant, helping people to listen and to apply the message as well as demonstrating the essential humanity of the preacher. It is on the other hand a very dangerous master.

Yet these verses speak of a refreshment of spirit that even the well-travelled apostle and his associates needed. In 1 Corinthians 16:18 Paul refers to a group of itinerant believers who had brought him refreshment in spirit and, as such, deserved recognition. All Christian workers will testify to the value of this encouraging ministry. Titus had gone out in faith, bolstered by Paul's assurances. It was probably his first visit to this notorious city and so he would need the comfort of the fellowship of believers. It has been my privilege to travel to, and preach in, some twenty countries overseas, often involving long and complicated itineraries, regularly preaching by interpretation with its hazards for preacher and translator alike! How important has been the joy of genuine, thoughtful, and often self-sacrificing care on the part of host Christians so that the giver in service becomes the receiver of blessing.

● *How have you refreshed and blessed your church leaders recently?*

● *What part can you play in helping your leaders flourish spiritually? Does the behaviour of the Corinthians towards Paul offer any insights?*

Titus had returned fully refreshed after his arduous journey and with the testimony of v15. The obedience of the Corinthian Christians, with its note of awesome respect is all the more remarkable when chapter 8 is read with its

96 *Rhythm of the Gospel*

challenge, especially in verse 6, to get on with fulfilling their financial promises. Few things are more calculated to destroy harmony than sermons or discussions on giving. The Bible often majors on issues we prefer to soft pedal for the sake of peace. Sex and money are two such issues. Perhaps if we took more risks and dared to confront people with the challenge of tithing, of putting God and his kingdom first, in how we spend our money, not only would Christian ventures get a new lease of life but also a new spirit of openness would prevail (read 1 Tim. 6: 6-10; 17-19).

As the world becomes smaller, communications more immediate, and travel less demanding, we have a great opportunity to discover the refreshment and blessings that come from the interchange of personnel and cultures within the world-wide family of God. It is an anticipation of the glory of heaven, with all nations and languages worshipping the Lamb and an extension of the wonder of Pentecost with its reversal of the tower of Babel. So at the Keswick Convention, birthplace of missionary movements and societies in the past, the new world view is seen in preachers from all continents, students and Christian leaders from many parts of the world united under the banner of ' all one in Christ Jesus'. How refreshing is this reality when contrasted with a divided, fragmented, hostile world into which we return and which we seek prayerfully to transform.

A MINISTRY OF REJOICING

We are back to the theme of Psalm 126 with its post-exilic note. Just as Israel discovered that the blessings of returning to the Promised Land only happened when the people gave priority to God's house, following the very straight preaching of Haggai, so Paul's experience with the Corinthian church had the same pattern of sowing in tears

Ministry of encouragement

and reaping in joy. That lies behind his words in verses 5-9. With his usual disarming honesty the apostle speaks of his restless spirit until Titus came back with good news. As Paul says he experienced 'conflicts on the outside, fears within' (v5). Yet these are not just the battles that can keep a person back from commitment; they remain part and parcel of the Christian experience, not least for the caring pastor. Elsewhere in this letter Paul speaks of 'the care of all the churches'. He knew what it was to weep with those who weep and rejoice with those who rejoice. He also knew what it was to weep for those who ought to weep but cared not. There is a real danger in our computerised society that people, even in Christian fellowships, become names seen on a screen but not people in whom the pastor has invested time and tears. We need to learn more of the spirit of Jesus who not only wept at the grave of his friend Lazarus but also outside the city walls of recalcitrant Jerusalem.

In verse 6 there is one of the many occurrences in the New Testament of the phrase 'but God', changing the complexion of the whole situation. Pastor Paul can speak of the comfort brought by the arrival of Titus with good news from Corinth so that verse 7 can end with the testimony that 'my joy was greater than ever'. He sees this as part of the ministry of God 'who comforts the downcast' and so we are reminded of the chain which brings joy into tense situations. The Corinthians welcomed Titus; Titus passes on the news to Paul; Paul is 'over the moon' and commits his feelings to a document that is still alive and active.

● *Consider the following scenarios that might be typical of your church. How could you best comfort the downcast?*
  – *A woman whose Christian husband has left her and wants a divorce.*
  – *A family who have had to return home from the mission field because their visas have not been renewed.*

Rhythm of the Gospel

- *A Christian friend who has been badly hurt by the words and actions of another believer.*
- *Paul talks of my 'joy knows no bounds' (v4) and my 'joy was greater that ever' (v7). What is the key to experiencing such joy in difficult times?*

We all desperately want shortcuts. From time to time in my itinerant ministry on busy roads I have tried to avoid traffic jams, frustration and incipient road rage by trying some apparent alternative detour, only to find worse problems such as getting completely lost or hitting some cul-de-sac. Then the last state is worse than the first. In Christian experience many love to espouse superficial but tantalisingly attractive quick fixes with excitement, new manifestations and ministry that titillate the emotions without engaging the mind in disciplined thinking and the will in determined action. But the alternative is not necessarily a dead intellectual exercise and drab worship. Ultimately, historic biblical Christianity offers joy with pain. In John 16:21 Jesus uses the analogy of the pangs of giving birth being subsumed in the exhilarating joy of new life. You cannot have one without the other.

- *'Christianity offers joy with pain'; explain and give further examples of this statement.*
- *If Christianity doesn't offer unalloyed joy, how can Jesus' statement in John 10:10 'I have come that they may have life, and have it to the full' be true?*

Soon the apostle will move, in the strength of his renewed confidence in the Corinthian Christians, to challenge them about giving from their material well being to the Jerusalem church that is now facing financial problems. He sees this not as merely pragmatic justice but even more a demonstration of the gospel at work in individuals and in the church. It is all part of the rhythm of the gospel at

Ministry of encouragement

work. Rhythm brings harmony, joy and satisfaction. From the good news of God at work in a Christian community comes the good news of what Christ has done for us all. Mission is the life-blood of the church in every age and any ministry worthy of the name will begin, be renewed, and be completed in mission, remembering only that such mission is never-ending with the unfinished task awaiting every gospel man and woman in every age.

FURTHER STUDY

Consider characters from the Old and New Testaments. How have they exhibited godly and worldly sorrow? What can we learn from them about the kind of attitudes and behaviour we should adopt?

REFLECTION AND RESPONSE

Who do you identify with?

- Are you like the Corinthians? Have you sincerely repented of some sin and been reconciled with another believer? Have you experienced godly sorrow and are now eager to be involved in Christian service again?

- Are you like Titus? Have you recently been blessed by another Christian, have you been encouraged by their generosity and obedience to God? Have you been able to share that blessing with others?

- Are you like Paul? Have you had a confrontation with another Christian and been anxious about the outcome? Have you experienced real joy as you watched other Christians flourish?

As you reflect on where you are on this cycle of repentance, refreshment and rejoicing, consider what God is teaching you. How does he want you to grow spiritually in this phase of your life, in these particular circumstances? Think back over the ways the Corinthians, Titus and Paul were encouraged. Follow their example and chose one way that you will try and encourage someone else to flourish spiritually this week.

REVIEW 2 CORINTHIANS 2:13-7:16

Re-read the whole section at one sitting. As you read aloud, pause occasionally and give the group time to mention the key themes and issues that arise from the text. Have a scribe write down your thoughts. Then put these thoughts in the form of a question. Choose a couple of questions to discuss together and make personal applications. Below are a few questions to help you get started:

- What aroma of Christ do people get when they spend time with me?
- What commends my Christian life to others?
- What proof is there of my devotion to Christ?
- Where does my confidence in ministry come from?
- In what ways am I becoming more like Jesus?
- How will I encourage myself not to lose heart and give up the faith?
- Does my presentation of the gospel preserve the integrity of the message?
- What are my eyes fixed on?
- Is it really all the same to me if I am in heaven with God or serving him on earth?
- Am I reconciled to God and to other Christians?
- Despite the hardships of my life am I still open hearted with other believers?
- In what ways am I unsuitably yoked to an unbeliever?
- Do I need to repent of a particular sin?
- Am I joyful and bringing joy and encouragement to others?

POINTS TO PONDER

- What have you learnt about God?
- What have you learnt about yourself?
- What actions or attitudes do you need to change as a result?